Eugene C. Sommer

Perfect Love

J. A. WOOD

Abridged by
John Paul, D.D.

BEACON HILL PRESS
Kansas City, Missouri

FIRST PRINTING, 1944
SECOND PRINTING, 1944
THIRD PRINTING, 1947
FOURTH PRINTING, 1949
FIFTH PRINTING, 1950

PRINTED IN THE UNITED STATES OF AMERICA

CONTENTS

FROM THE AUTHOR'S ORIGINAL PREFACE

The following pages are designed for the benefit of believers in the church of Christ, who "hunger and thirst after righteousness," and seek light concerning the *doctrine, experience, profession,* and *practice* of Christian holiness.

The book retains its catechetical form, to meet the many interrogations so often made regarding this subject, and also to help the memory of the reader. This form allows a general, though brief, presentation of the whole subject. Our object has been to *clearly* present, and *strongly* enforce gospel truth, and when we could do this more efficiently in the *language of others,* and by quotations from them, we have freely done so.

We have given credit for what we have selected, except in those cases where we have changed the words or phrases. *The italics in some quotations are our own.* The reader will find many things in this work, which, in their original forms, are dispersed through many volumes, which most people have neither money to purchase nor time to read.

We have not written so much for the learnedly critical, as for the *common people* who need "line upon line, and precept upon precept." Many of these appear perplexed and mystified on this plain and intelligible subject; which, when properly understood, is seen to possess none of those objectionable features which are so often attributed to it by its mistaken opponents.

Perfect Love

TERMS SIGNIFYING COMPLETE GOSPEL SALVATION

1. *What terms are commonly used to express full salvation?*

The Scripture terms are, *"perfect love," "perfection," "sanctification,"* and *"holiness."* These terms are synonymous, all pointing to the same precious state of grace. While they denote the same religious state, each one of them indicates some essential characteristic, and hence these terms are significantly expressive of full salvation.

The word *"sanctify,"* and its derivatives, occur in the Scriptures, with reference to men and things, over *one hundred times.* The term *"perfection"* signifies completeness of Christian character; its freedom from all sin, and possession of all the graces of the Spirit, *complete in kind.* "Let us go on unto *perfection."* The word *"perfection"* and its relatives, occur *one hundred and one times* in the Scriptures. In over fifty of these instances it is predicated of human character under the operation of grace. The term *"holiness"* is more generic and comprehensive than the others, including salvation from sin, and the possession of the image and spirit of God. To be holy is to be *whole, entire,* or *perfect* in a moral sense, and in ordinary use is synonymous with purity and godliness. "Follow peace with all men, and holiness without which no man shall see the Lord." The word *"holy"* and its derivatives, occur not less than *one hundred and twenty times* in their application to men and things. The word *"justify"* and its derivatives, occur *seventy-four* times in regard to men; and the word *"pardon"* with its derivatives, in their application to penitent sinners, occur only *seventeen times.*

The phrase *"perfect love"* is expressive of the spirit and temper, or moral atmosphere in which the wholly sanctified and perfect Christian lives. "He that dwelleth in love dwelleth in God, and God in him"; and, "Herein is our love made perfect."

2. *Are not these terms applicable to the beginning of the Christian life?*

They are not usually, and some of them are never so applied. There is a sense in which all Christians are denominated holy, and sanctified; and the terms "holiness," and "sanctification," with their derivatives, are occasionally applied in the Scriptures to the merely regenerate, as when a part is put for the whole, a thing not uncommon in the Bible. All Christians are *pardoned,* therefore *legally* holy; they are *regenerated,* which is holiness begun, and are holy in a *general sense* as compared with their former condition. The terms used in the Scriptures to express the commencement of the Christian life, are, "born of God," "born again," "born of the Spirit," "converted," and "regeneration."

SECTION II

3. What is Justification?

Justification is pardon or forgiveness. Sin is a violation of law, and is a *capital offense.* "The wages of sin is death." Justification is that governmental act of God's grace, absolving the penitent sinner from all past guilt, and removing the penalty of violated law. It precedes regeneration, and is by faith. The penitent sinner believes on the Lord Jesus Christ, and God pardons his sins, remits the punishment they deserve, receives him into favor and fellowship, and treats him as though he had not sinned. "Being justified by faith, we have peace with God through our Lord Jesus Christ." Rom. 5:1.

4. Can a state of justification be retained while sin is committed?

It cannot. "He that committeth sin is of the devil." The commission of sin negatives the justified state, and any professing Christian who lives in the commission of sin, *is a sinner* and not a saint. "He that saith, I know him, and keepeth not his commandments, *is a liar.*"—"We know that whosoever is born of God *sinneth not.*"

The lowest type of a Christian sinneth not, and is not condemned. The *minimum* of salvation is salvation from *sinning.* The *maximum* is salvation from *pollution*—the inclination to sin.

Mr. Wesley says: "But even babes in Christ are so far perfect as not to *commit* sin. . . . We all agree and earnestly maintain, 'He that *committeth* sin is of *the devil.*' We agree, 'Whosoever is born of God doth not commit sin'."—*Sermon on "Sin in Believers."*

9

"The *continuance* of the *justified* state," says Bishop Peck, "implies *obedience* in *intention* to *all* the *requirements* of the gospel, the law of progress ('grow in grace'), and the law of purity ('be ye holy'), included."—*Central Idea*, p. 59.

Rev. Albert Barnes says: "No man can be a Christian who voluntarily indulges in sin, or in what he knows to be wrong."—*Notes on II Corinthians*, chap. 7.

The conditions of receiving justification and of retaining it are the same. Christ is received by penitential submission and faith. "As ye have therefore received Christ Jesus the Lord, *so* walk ye in him." Justification cannot be retained with less consecration and faith than that by which it was received.

Conscious *confidence* and conscious *guilt* cannot coexist in the same heart. There is a vital union between justifying faith and an obedient spirit. While obedience makes faith perfect, disobedience destroys it. Salvation is by appropriating faith, and such faith or trust can be exercised only when there is a consciousness of complete surrender to God. A justified state can exist only in connection with a serious, honest intention to obey all the commands of God.

We should make a distinction, to some extent, between sin committed by deliberate thought and set purpose, and sin committed by sudden impulse, under strong distraction and temptation.

5. *Are obedience and disobedience units respectively in their spirit and root?*

They are; and they are eternal antagonisms.

The real spirit of disobedience is ever one and the same —the same for every precept, for all times, and for all circumstances. Each sin, alike, is a violation of the same obligations, outrages the same law, insults the same Lawgiver, evinces the same rebellion of spirit, and incurs the same fearful curse pronounced against the lawbreaker. "Whosoever shall keep the whole law, and yet offend in one point, he is guilty of all" (James 2:10).

The real spirit of obedience is ever *one and the same,* the same for *every precept,* the same for all times, and for all circumstances. The spirit of true obedience has regard to God's supreme authority, and involves submission of the whole soul to that authority. Every act of real obedience has reference to the same obligations, regard for the same law, respect for the same Lawgiver, evinces the same submissive spirit, and secures the same gracious reward in the divine favor and blessing. "He that is faithful in that which is least, is faithful also in much" (Luke 16:10).

A *spirit of disobedience* in the heart, in regard to any item of God's will, vitiates for the time any true obedience.

SECTION III

6. *What is Regeneration—its nature and extent?*

Regeneration is the impartation of spiritual life to the human soul, in which God imparts, organizes, and calls into being the capabilities, attributes, and functions of the new nature. It is a change from death to life, from the dominion of sin to the reign of grace, and restores the spiritual life which was lost by the fall. It is instantaneously wrought by the Holy Spirit, and always accompanies justification.

Rev. Luther Lee says: Regeneration is a *renewal* of our fallen nature by the power of the Holy Spirit, received through faith in Jesus Christ, whereby the regenerate are delivered from the *power* of sin which *reigns* over all the *unregenerate*.

Bishop Foster says: Regeneration is a work done in us, in the way of changing our inward nature; a work by which a *spiritual life* is infused into the soul, whereby he (the regenerate) brings forth the peaceable fruits of righteousness, *has victory over sin,* is enabled to *resist corrupt tendencies,* and has peace and joy in the Holy Ghost.

7. *What is the difference between justification and sanctification?*

Justification secures our adoption into the family of God, our sonship, our heirship, and our spiritual affiliation; sanctification secures a preparation or meetness for "the inheritance of the saints in light." The former makes the believer *a child of God,* while the latter im-

12

parts *the image of God.* The first secures a title to heav-
en, and the second a preparation for it.

Justification is an instantaneous and complete act; it
has no degrees, all who are justified are freely and fully
justified "through the redemption in Christ Jesus"; sanctification has degrees, some are *partially,* and some are
entirely sanctified. The *beginning,* and the *completion*
of sanctification are both instantaneously wrought. The
approach to entire sanctification may be gradual.

Justification, God's act, and sanctification, God's work,
are *experimentally* by faith, *meritoriously* by the blood of
Christ, *instrumentally* by the word of God, and *efficiently*
by the Holy Ghost. See John 17:17; I John 1:7; Rom.
15:16; I Tim. 4:5.

SECTION IV

8. Do the Scriptures teach a distinction between regeneration and entire sanctification?

They do. "And I, brethren, could not speak unto you as unto spiritual, but as unto *carnal,* even as unto babes in Christ. For ye are yet *carnal;* for whereas there is among you *envying,* and *strife,* and *divisions,* are ye not carnal, and walk as men?" "Having, therefore, these promises, dearly beloved, let us cleanse ourselves from all *filthiness* of the *flesh* and *spirit, perfecting holiness* in the fear of God." "And the very God of peace *sanctify* you *wholly.*" "Sanctify them through thy truth; thy word is truth." All these passages have reference to Christians in a regenerated state, but not entirely sanctified.

9. Does the Christian Church generally recognize this distinction?

It does. "By a consent almost universal," says Rev. Dr. Hodge, "the word regeneration is now used to designate, not the whole work of sanctification."—"According to the Scriptures, and the undeniable evidence of history, regeneration does not remove all sin."—*Systematic Theology,* vol. III, p. 290.

Professor Upham says: "The distinction which is made in the Scriptures between the two is regarded so obvious and incontrovertible by most writers, that it has naturally passed as an established truth into treatises on theology." —*Interior Life.*

10. Does the Methodist Church teach a distinction?

She does very clearly in her Discipline, Catechism, Hymn Book, and by all her standard authorities.

14

All the leading writers and standard authorities of Methodism teach a distinction. Mr. Wesley might be quoted very largely. He says: "Sanctification begins in the moment a man is justified. Yet sin remains in him, yea, the seed of all sin, till he is sanctified throughout."

Rev. Richard Watson says: "That a distinction exists between a regenerate state and a state of entire and perfect holiness, will be generally allowed."—*Institutes*, Part II, chap. 29.

Rev. John Fletcher says: "We do not deny that the remains of the *carnal mind* still cleave to imperfect Christians." "This fault, corruption or infection, doth remain in them who are regenerated."—*Last Check*, pp. 507-541.

11. *Does this distinction harmonize with Christian experience?*

It does. All Christians are regenerated, while but few claim to be sanctified wholly. The penitent sinner seeks for pardon and acceptance, and is not concerned for the blessing of perfect love, or entire sanctification. After regeneration, the more clearly the light of justification shines, the more the converted soul will see its indwelling sin, and feel the necessity of entire sanctification.

12. *Does the Lord ever entirely sanctify the soul at justification and regeneration?*

We do not know. Possibly this may be the case in some instances, but, certainly, is not the usual order of God. In all our acquaintance with many thousands of the purest and best Christians in all the various churches, we have yet to find a clear case of entire sanctification at conversion. While multitudes claim that their souls have been cleansed from all sin subsequent to their justification, we do not recollect a single instance of a distinct witness of entire sanctification at conversion.

Mr. Wesley says: "But we *do not know a single instance,* in any place, of a person's receiving in one and the same moment remission of sins, the abiding witness of the Spirit, and a new and a clean heart."—*Plain Account,* p. 34.

Dr. Clarke says: "I have been twenty-three years a traveling preacher, and have been acquainted with some thousands of Christians during that time, who were in different states of grace; and I never, to my knowledge, met with a single instance where God both *justified* and *sanctified at the same time.*"—*Everett's Life of Dr. A. Clarke.*

13. *How did Mr. Wesley view the idea that the soul is entirely sanctified at regeneration?*

"I cannot therefore by any means receive this assertion, that there is no sin in a believer from the moment he is justified—

"1. Because it is contrary to the whole tenor of Scripture.

"2. Because it is contrary to the experience of the children of God.

"3. Because it is absolutely new, never heard of in the world till yesterday.

"4. Because it is naturally attended with the most fatal consequences; not only grieving those whom God hath not grieved, but, perhaps, dragging them into everlasting perdition."—*Sermons,* Vol. I, p. 111.

14. *What was the Moravian or Zinzendorf doctrine which Mr. Wesley opposed?*

That the soul is entirely sanctified when it is justified; that regeneration, which takes place at the time of justification, is identical with entire sanctification.

It was this error that occasioned the writing and publication of his sermon on "Sin in Believers."

He says in his Journal: "I retired to Lewisham, and wrote the sermon on 'Sin in Believers,' in order to remove a mistake, which some were laboring to propagate—that there is no sin in any that are justified."—*Works,* Vol. IV, p. 147.

15. *Is the theory that the soul is entirely sanctified at regeneration, attended with serious difficulties?*

It is. It involves the whole subject of Christian sanctification in inextricable difficulties. The following are some of them:

If sanctification is complete at justification, then every man who enjoys religion is entirely sanctified; every Christian, to be truthful, should *profess* entire sanctification and all the directions in the word of God, to seek holiness, sanctification, or perfect love, are given exclusively to sinners.

If sanctification is complete at justification, then converts are not to seek for any further cleansing, ministers have no right to urge *Christians* to "go on unto perfection," or to "cleanse themselves from all filthiness of the flesh and spirit, perfecting holiness in the fear of God," and all who feel the fruits of the flesh are in a state of condemnation.

A system involving such difficulties cannot be received as the truth of God, and should be regarded as antiscriptural, and avoided as dangerous heresy.

16. *If regeneration is partial and not entire sanctification, where is the limit?*

Rev. B. W. Gorham: "The infant, and the man in a state of assured justification before God, are alike parties to the covenant of grace, which entitles them to holiness and heaven. Both are alike free from any voluntary antagonism to holiness; and should death come suddenly to both, our covenant-keeping Lord will surely perfect that which is lacking in each, even in the very article of death."— *God's Method with Man,* p. 57.

17. *Does a state of justification involve a desire to be holy?*

It does. If a man is a Christian, and in a justified state, he has the heart of a child of God, and desires to render him a *present, full*, and *unreserved obedience*. This is implied in the very nature of true religion. A desire for holiness is a *spontaneity* of the regenerate heart, and the Christian who argues against holiness will get down on his knees and pray for a clean heart—his regenerated heart getting the better of his head.

Bishop Peck says: "Regeneration in its lowest state loves holiness, and pants to be filled with it."

SECTION V

18. *How soon after regeneration may the soul be entirely sanctified?*

There is no time stated in the Scriptures which must elapse after conversion before the soul can be entirely sanctified. The only prerequisite to the seeking of holiness is the justified and regenerate state. Even "babes in Christ" are exhorted "to go on unto perfection"; and all believers are included in the command, "Be ye holy, for I am holy." The declaration, "It is the will of God, even your sanctification," is true of every believer, and was originally addressed to heathen converts who were but babes in Christ.

When first converted, we should press on into this goodly land which flows with milk and honey. When the kingdom of God is first set up in our hearts, the course is short, the difficulties are comparatively few, and we cannot be too *early*, or too much in *earnest*, seeking purity.

Rev. John Wesley says: "I have been lately thinking a good deal on one point, wherein, perhaps, we have all been wanting. We have not made it a *rule, as soon as ever persons are justified, to remind them of 'going on unto perfection.'* WHEREAS THIS IS THE VERY TIME PREFERABLE TO ALL OTHERS. They have then the simplicity of little children; and they are fervent in spirit, ready to cut off a right hand or pluck out the right eye. But if we once suffer this fervor to subside, we shall find it hard enough to bring them again even to this point."—*Letter to Thomas Rankin.*

THE NATURE OF CHRISTIAN PERFECTION

19. *What is entire sanctification or Christian perfection?*

Negatively, it is that state of grace which excludes all sin from the heart. *Positively,* it is the possession of pure love to God. "Blessed are the pure in heart." "The blood of Jesus Christ, his Son, cleanseth us from all sin." "Love is the fulfilling of the law." "The end of the commandment is love out of a pure heart." In the grace of justification, sins, as *acts* of transgression, are *pardoned.* In the grace of sanctification, sin, as a malady, is *removed,* so that the heart is pure.

Mr. Wesley says: "Both my brother [Charles Wesley] and I maintain, that Christian perfection is that love of God and our neighbor which implies DELIVERANCE FROM ALL SIN."

"It is the loving God with all our heart, mind, soul, and strength. This implies that no wrong temper, none contrary to love, remains in the soul; and that all the thoughts, words, and actions are governed by pure love." —Vol. VI, p. 500.

Rev. John Fletcher says: "It is the *pure* love of God and man shed abroad in a faithful believer's heart by the Holy Ghost given unto him, to *cleanse* him, and to *keep him clean.*"

Dr. A. Clarke: "What, then, is this complete sanctification? It is the cleansing of the blood, that has not been cleansed; it is *washing the soul of a true believer from the remains of sin.*"—*Clarke's Theology,* p. 206.

The German United Brethren Church say: "By perfect holiness we understand the separation and purification from all inhering sin, after regeneration, by the blood of Jesus Christ, the Son of God; and the filling of the heart with the love of God by the Holy Ghost."

Rev. Wm. McDonald says: "It is the removal from our moral natures, through faith in Christ, of all sinful desires and tempers—all pride, anger, envy, unbelief, and love of the world; and the possession in these purified natures of the unmixed graces of faith, humility, resignation, patience, meekness, self-denial, and love."—*Scriptural Views*, p. 23.

Noah Webster defines sanctification—"The act of making holy, . . . the *state* of being *thus purified* or sanctified." "To sanctify, in a general sense, is to cleanse, purify, or make holy, . . . *to cleanse from corruption, to purify from sin.*"

20. *What is the distinction between regeneration and entire sanctification?*

The first includes, in addition to imparted spiritual life, the *commencement* of purification; the other is the possession of the same spiritual life with *complete* purification.

The regenerate state and the fully sanctified state differ in moral quality; grace and life in one case have antagonisms in the heart—in the other they have none. The "new life," or "new man," exists in an *uncleansed* soul in the former case, and in a *purified* soul in the latter. In the regenerate there is the *new life unto righteousness*, but not the *complete death unto sin.* In the entirely sanctified, the new life with all the graces of the Spirit exist in a *pure heart.*

Mr. Wesley says: "That believers are delivered from the *guilt* and *power* of sin we allow; that they are delivered from the *being* of it we deny. . . . Christ, indeed, cannot *reign* where sin *reigns;* neither will he *dwell* where sin is *allowed.* But he *is* and *dwells* in the heart of every

believer who is *fighting against all sin,* although it be not
yet *purified.* . . . Indeed this grand point, that there are
two contrary principles in [unsanctified] believers—*nature* and *grace,* the *flesh* and the *spirit*—runs through all
the Epistles of St. Paul, yea, through all the Holy Scriptures; almost all the directions and exhortations therein
are founded on this supposition, pointing at wrong *tempers* or *practices* in those who are notwithstanding acknowledged by the inspired writers to be believers."—
Sermon on Sin in Believers.

Rev. Richard Watson says: "In this regenerate state,
the former *corruptions* of the *heart* may remain and *strive*
for the *mastery;* but that which characterizes and dis-
tinguishes it from the state of a penitent before justification, before he is in Christ, is, that they are not even his
inward habit, and that they have no dominion."—*Institutes,* Vol. II, p. 450.

21. *Is there a difference between sin and depravity?*

There is, a very important difference.

1. Sin is "the transgression of the law," and involves
moral action, either by voluntary *omission,* or willful
commission, and it always incurs guilt.

2. Depravity is a *state* or *condition,* a defilement or
perversity of spirit. It is developed in the soul, in inclinations to sin, or in *sinward tendencies.*

3. Sin, strictly speaking, is voluntary, and involves
responsible action, and is a thing to be *pardoned.*

4. Depravity is *inborn, inherited,* and *inbred.* It is
derived from fallen Adam, and is augmented by actual
sin.

5. All sin involves *guilt,* depravity does not, unless it
be assented to, yielded to, cherished, or its cure willfully
neglected.

6. Depravity is one of the *results* of sin, and it may
have somewhat of the nature of sin, in the sense of being

a *disconformity* or *unlikeness* to God; and it is in this sense that "all unrighteousness is sin."

22. *Do those merely regenerated often think indwelling sin is destroyed?*

They do; and this is frequently the case when the soul is first converted. Not infrequent, the transition from nature to grace, from death to life, and from darkness to light, is so marked, and the love and gladness of the new-born soul is so overflowing, as for the time to make the impression the whole heart is cleansed.

"How naturally do those who experience such a change [regeneration] imagine that all sin is gone, that it is entirely rooted out of their hearts, and has no more place therein! How easily do they draw that inference, 'I feel no sin, therefore I have none; it does not stir, therefore it does not exist; it has no motion, therefore it has no being!' But it is seldom long before they are undeceived, finding sin was only *suspended* not *destroyed*."—*Wesley's Sermons*, Vol. I, p. 385.

23. *What is the cause of so much prejudice against the doctrine of entire Sanctification, and even of hostility to it?*

1. The doctrine is misunderstood. Multitudes misapprehended its true nature. It is often taken to mean more than is intended, and more than is taught.

2. The doctrine and experience of entire sanctification has been prejudiced among common people by being frequently identified with *culture, social refinement,* and the *highest finish;* then of course it can be possessed only by the few who have the time, the means, and the opportunity to obtain the highest *development* and *brightest polish,* and *cultivation.*

3. Many of our ministers are at fault in this matter, in not seeking this blessed experience themselves; for not studying and mastering the subject; and for not preach-

ing it more *clearly, strongly,* and *explicitly* to the people.

4. Much of the prejudice and opposition to this doctrine comes from remaining depravity in unsanctified believers. Indwelling sin is an antagonism to holiness, and, in so far as any Christian has *inbred sin,* he has *within him* opposition to holiness.

24. *Is Christian Perfection absolute perfection?*

It is not. We know of no writer who has ever taught any such perfection in man. God's moral perfections are like an infinite ocean, as boundless and fathomless as immensity. Up to this perfection neither man, nor angel, nor seraph can ever come. Between the highest degree of human perfection, and the perfection of God, there is the difference between the *finite* and the *infinite.* Absolute perfection belongs to God alone. In this sense, "there is none good but one, that is God." The highest, sweetest, and most lovely angel in Paradise is infinitely below absolute perfection.

25. *Is Christian perfection the same as Angelic perfection?*

It is not. Angels are a higher order of intelligences; they are innocent and sinlessly pure. The fire of their love burns with an intensity, and their services are performed with a precision and rectitude not possible to mortals. In this world we must be content with *Christian perfection;* when we reach heaven we shall be "equal unto the angels." Christian perfection or holiness is a perfection according to the capacity of a man, and not according to the capacity of an angel, or a glorified saint.

26. *Is Christian perfection synonymous with Adamic perfection?*

It is not. There is a wide difference between a pure-hearted Christian saved by grace, and unfallen Adam in his Paradisiacal glory; a difference in *range of powers, innocency,* and *grounds of justification.* Adam was justified by works, and was free from the broken powers, and infirmities of fallen human nature.

Every creature of God may be perfect after its *kind,* and according to its *degree.* Angels, cherubim, and seraphim are all perfect, but their perfection falls infinitely below the absolute perfection of God. There is a gradation which belongs to all the works of God, and hence there are various sorts and degrees of perfection.

Christian perfection is a *perfection of love, pure* love in a *fallen* but *purified soul.*

Mr. Wesley adopted the term *perfection* because he found it in the Scriptures; (see question 1;) he deemed St. Paul and St. John sufficient authorities for its use. The Christian world has also largely recognized the term in the writings of Clement, Macarius, Kempis, Fenelon, Lucas, and many other writers both Papal and Protestant.

27. *Do you teach a sinless perfection?*

If by sinless perfection be meant *infallibility,* or a state in which the soul *cannot sin,* we answer, No. John Wesley says: "Therefore *sinless* perfection is a phrase I never use, lest I should seem to contradict myself. I believe a person filled with the love of God is still liable to these involuntary transgressions. Such transgressions you may call sins, if you please; I do not."—*Plain Account,* p. 67.

If by this phrase be meant, a perfect observance of the evangelical law of love, so as to love God with all the heart, soul, and strength, we answer, by the grace of God, *Yes.* See Deuteronomy 30:6.

28. *Does Christian Perfection exclude a need of the atonement?*

No; not for a moment. All Christian life is in Christ; and is dependent upon Him, as the branch upon the vine.

"I am the vine, ye are the branches. . . . Without me ye can do nothing." The pure in heart abide in Christ, by a *continuous faith,* which is the vital bond of union with him. Christ does not give life to the soul *separate from,* but *in* and *with himself.*

Dr. Clarke observes: "No more can an effect subsist without its cause, than a sanctified soul abide in holiness without the indwelling Sanctifier."—*Clarke's Theology,* p. 187.

29. *What does the highest evangelical perfection include?*

Under the economy of grace, the measure of man's responsibility and obedience is his actual ability, as a fallen and infirm being, and not the ability of an unfallen being. The commands, "To love the Lord thy God with all thy heart," and to "Be perfect as your Father in heaven is perfect," are to be interpreted in harmony with this view; the Father being the human standard only in *purity* or *holiness,* and not in range of powers or natural perfections.

The highest evangelical perfection embraces two things: A perfection of *love,* proportioned to the powers of each individual, and a steady progress in love harmonizing with our circumstances and increasing capacity and ability.

Let it be remembered, God does not require any more than we can actually do through grace. As we can give no more than our all, he requires no more. The divine requirement to love him with *all our heart,* is adapted to all periods and all intelligences; it is a claim of both Testaments, and binding under all dispensations.

30. *If the law is uncompromising in its claims, and the best Christians defective, because of powers enfeebled by the fall, how can men be perfect?*

Legal perfection is one thing, and evangelical Christian perfection is another.

Under the evangelical law of grace, *"Love is the fulfilling of the law."* Although our powers are impaired by the fall, St. Paul says: "What the law could not do, in that it was weak through the flesh, God sending his own Son in the likeness of sinful flesh, and for sin condemned sin in the flesh; that *the righteousness of the law might be fulfilled in us,* who walk not after the flesh, but after the spirit."

The fulfillment of the law was epitomized by our Saviour—"Thou shalt love the Lord thy God with all thy heart, and with all thy soul, and with all thy strength, and thy neighbor as thyself"; and, "On these two hang all the law and the prophets." Grace to observe this is provided, and promised in the Old Testament—"The Lord thy God will circumcise [purify] thine heart, and the heart of thy seed, to love the Lord thy God with all thine heart, and with all thy soul, that thou mayest live" (Deut. 30:6).

31. *Is personal holiness imparted or imputed by Christ?*

We know of no *imputed* holiness. Christ *imparts* and never *imputes* holiness. His righteousness never covers up a corrupt heart. He never apologizes for sin, nor throws a mantle over it. It is to be feared, many who are living in sin are cherishing the delusion that they "are complete in Christ," through an imaginary imputed holiness, while they fail to seek personal righteousness in his cleansing blood. It is a pernicious Antinomian heresy to trust in Christ's imputed righteousness instead of seeking and receiving personal redemption through his blood. We must be made "partakers of his holiness."

Our perfection is *in Christ,* as the perfection of the branch is in the vine. Grace is derived from Christ only by a union with him, as the branch to the vine. "Christ in you the hope of glory"—dwelling in us by the Holy Spirit, and sanctifying us by his blood. Christ atones, intercedes, and procures blessings for us, and of God is made unto us "wisdom, righteousness, sanctification, and redemption."

32. *Is repression entire sanctification?*

It is not. Inward *repression* is not inward *purity*.

The justified and regenerate state holds in subjection remaining depravity, so that it does not reign. Of the justified believer Mr. Wesley says: "He has power, both over *outward* and *inward* sin, even from the moment he is justified."—Vol. I, p. 109.

Choking down and repressing indwelling sin, is not the process of cleansing the heart. "Wash me, and I shall be whiter than snow." *Repression* is not *washing*. The inward impurities *repressed* in regeneration, are *removed* by entire sanctification. Repressive power is nowhere ascribed to the blood of Christ, but purgative, cleansing efficacy.

33. *Does Christian Perfection exclude growth in grace?*

By no means. The pure in heart grow *faster* than any others. We believe in no state of grace excluding *progression*, either in this world or in heaven, but expect to grow with increasing rapidity forever. It is the same with the soul wholly sanctified as with the regenerate: it must progress in order to retain the favor of God and the grace possessed. There is no standing still in a *religious life*, nor in a *sinful life*. We must either *progress* or *regress*.

34. *Can holiness be retained without growing in grace?*

It can only be retained by a steady progress in the divine life. The conditions of *obtaining* holiness and of *retaining* it are the same; and the conditions of obtaining and retaining it are those by which the soul is to grow and mature in holiness. Hence a violation of the conditions of increase and growth in holiness forfeits the state of holiness itself.

35. *How can holiness be perfect and yet progressive?*

Perfection in *quality* does not exclude increase in *quantity*. Beyond entire sanctification there is no increase in *purity*, as that which is pure cannot be more than pure; but there may be unlimited increase in *expansion* and *quantity*.

After love is made perfect, it may abound more and yet more. Holiness in the entirely sanctified soul is *exclusive*, and is perfect in *kind* or in *quality*, but is limited in *degree* or *quantity*. The capacities of the soul are expansive and progressive, and holiness in *measure* can increase corresponding to increasing capacity. Faith, love, humility, and patience, may be perfect in *kind*, and yet increase in *volume* and *power*, or in measure harmonizing with increasing capacity. A tree may be perfectly sound, healthy, and vigorous in its branches, leaves, and fruit, and yet year by year increase perpetually its capacity and fruitfulness.

36. *Where is growth in grace to be chiefly?*

Subsequent to entire sanctification. A vast majority of church-members appear to think, between regeneration and entire sanctification must be a lifetime of growth in grace. This is a serious mistake, and we fear has overthrown millions. It is unscriptural to teach growth as a substitute for cleansing.

Mr. Wesley says: "One perfected in love may grow in grace far swifter than he did before."—*Plain Account*, p. 167.

37. *Why can a soul entirely sanctified grow in grace more rapidly than others?*

Holiness does not put a finality to anything within us, except to the existence and practice of sin; and the soul, perfect in love, can grow faster than others:

1. Because all the internal antagonisms of growth are excluded from the heart. Indwelling sin is the greatest hindrance to growth in grace. When the weeds in a garden are exterminated, the vegetables will grow the more rapidly.

2. Because the purified heart has *stronger* faith, *clearer* light, is *nearer* the fountain, and dwells in a *purer atmosphere* than before it was cleansed.

3. Because after the Holy Ghost has cleansed the heart, He has a better chance than before to *enlighten, enrich, adorn,* and *renew* it, with more and more of *love* and *power.*

4. Because the *death of sin* gives free scope to the *life of righteousness.* The purified heart is a *pure moral soil,* where the *plants of righteousness,* the graces of the spirit, have an unobstructed growth.

5. Because the powers and capacities of the entirely sanctified soul increase and expand more rapidly than before, and with this increasing capacity there is a corresponding increase in the volume and power of the graces of the Spirit.

6. Because it perfects the *conditions* of the most thrifty and symmetrical growth possible in this life. Holiness is spiritual health. "By his stripes we are *healed.*" All disease and deformity obstruct growth, while health is its most essential condition.

Fletcher says: "A perfect Christian grows far more than a feeble believer, whose growth is still *obstructed* by the shady thorns of sin, and by the *draining suckers of iniquity.—Last Check,* p. 499.

38. *Do the graces of the Spirit exist in the entirely sanctified soul without alloy?*

They do. In the entirely sanctified they are perfect in *quality,* but are limited in *degree.* In the merely regenerate all the graces of the Spirit *numerically* exist, but they have more or less antagonism in the soul, in the risings, and perverse inclination of carnal nature. After the heart is cleansed these virtues are *exclusive,* and exist in *simplicity,* and are perfect in *quality.*

39. *Are there two kinds of religious life?*

There are not. There is but one kind of spiritual life, strictly speaking. The life, though divinely imparted, may exist in a *partially* purified heart, or in one *entirely* purified. The merely regenerate is possessed of both grace and inbred sin. Please note, however, these have existence in the same heart without forming a *combination* or *composition,* being *opposed* to each other, and possessed of no *affiliation.* There is no such *commingling* of grace and indwelling sin as to make an adulterated holiness. An *adulterated* holiness is an absurdity, a contradiction. *Holiness is holiness.* The apostle refers to this contrariety and antagonism in Galatians: "For the flesh lusteth against the spirit, and the spirit against the flesh, and these are contrary the one to the other."

40. *Does Christian perfection exclude a liability to temptation?*

It does not. Adam and Eve were tempted in Eden. Our Saviour was tempted. Temptation does not imply any *necessity* to sin, nor necessarily any tendency in the mind to sin. The fact that a man is tempted is no proof that he is *sinful* or *inclined to sin.* An unfelt trial is no trial, and pain of mind, in itself, is no more sin than pain of body. Even Jesus *"suffered* being tempted," (Heb. 2:18). If temptation is incompatible with holiness, then He was unholy. He had a long and bitter siege of temptation during forty days in the wilderness. He was tempted even to kneel down and worship the devil. He was "in all points tempted like as we are, *yet without sin."* If temptation is inconsistent with holiness, then Adam and Eve were unholy before their fall.

41. *Are the temptations of the entirely sanctified soul the same as those of persons merely regenerated?*

While they are *essentially* the same, yet the temptations of each are peculiar to themselves. The temptations of the entirely sanctified are usually *sharper* and *shorter* than others. They are also entirely from *without,* there being no foes *within* a sanctified heart; all is peaceful, friendly, and right there. The temptations of a sanctified soul find no *favorable response from within,* while those of the unsanctified do, more or less. In the one case, temptations find *corrupt inclinations* in the heart in their favor; in the other they find none.

42. *When does temptation end and sin begin?*

The object of temptation must exist *intellectually,* or there could be no temptation. The temptation may exist to this extent without sin, and hence evil suggestions presented to our minds, which have no effect upon our *desires* or *will,* are only temptations.

No temptation or evil suggestion to the mind becomes sin till it is cherished or tolerated. Sin consists in yielding to temptation. So long as the soul maintains its integrity, so that temptation finds no *sympathy* within, no sin is committed and the soul remains unharmed, no matter how protracted or severe the fiery trial may prove.

43. *Does Christian holiness exclude a liability to apostasy?*

It does not; but it renders apostasy much less probable. Perfect love makes a strong fortress of the heart; this fortress will be attacked, but is not as likely to be taken as without holiness. Holiness makes no one impeccable, although it possesses all the elements of strength and stability. A liability to sin and fall is an essential condition of probation. Holiness secures the safest possible condition on earth.

44. *Does Christian perfection secure perfect knowledge?*

It does not. We cannot know all things, neither in this world, nor in the world to come. Nor do angels, nor the highest orders in heaven, know all things. The perfect in love have a clearer *apprehension* of God, of his *presence,* and of spiritual things (other circumstances being equal), than any others.

45. *Does Christian perfection exclude the infirmities of human nature?*

It does not. Freedom from these is not to be expected in this world. We must wait for deliverance from these until this mortal puts on immortality. These infirmities, so numerous and various, are the common inheritance of humanity. They are not *sins;* they are innocent; and although they may be our misfortune, they are included in the *"all things"* which, by the grace and blessing of God, shall work together for our good. Christian perfection does admit of numberless infirmities and imperfections, such as slowness of understanding, errors of judgment, mistakes in practice, erratic imaginations, a treacherous memory.

46. *Is it important to distinguish between inbred sin and the innocent infirmities of fallen human nature?*

It is; otherwise we may on the one hand *blame* and afflict ourselves needlessly; or, on the other, *excuse* ourselves from blame when we are really *culpable.* An intelligent, faithful Christian will wisely discriminate between them, and seek the *extirpation* of the one, and patiently *endure* the burdens of the other. Mr. Wesley says: "Let those who do call them sins beware how they confound these defects with sins, properly so called."—*Plain Account,* p. 67.

St. Paul recognizes this distinction; he writes to Timothy, "Them that *sin rebuke* before all, that others may also fear"; and yet he writes to the Romans, "We that are strong should bear with the *infirmities* of the weak." Here are two plain commands; the first not to bear with *sins,* and the second to bear with *infirmities.*

47. *What are the distinguishing characteristics of perfect love?*

Perfect love is perfect in *quality.* It is pure love, it has no alloy; perfect in *quantity,* filling the heart. "Be ye filled with the Spirit." It is *constant.* If not constant, it is not perfect. There may not always be ecstatic joy, but there must always be a supreme preference for God.

Perfect love is *progressive* love. We may not always see we are progressing, but this does not disprove the fact. It casts out fear—all slavish, harmful fear, such as the guilty feel. It excludes all those *warring elements* from the unsanctified heart which *excite distressing* and slavish fear. It casts out the fear of man, of want, of death, of hell, and all slavish fear of God. "He that feareth is not made perfect in love." It does not cast out the fear of *caution,* or a *loving, filial fear of God.* It induces this kind of fear. It guards against presumption on the one hand, and against despondency on the other. Perfect love brings out more fully and clearly the *evidences* of our regeneration, justification, and salvation. It enables the soul to realize more nearly and fully the *presence* and *blessedness* of Christ.

48. *Is perfect love or purity a very high state of grace?*

It is not. Though a blessed and glorious state, yet, when compared to "the *breadth,* and *length,* and *depth,* and *height,*" to which the soul may attain through the rich and abundant grace of God, it is not a very high state of grace. To be cleansed from all sin is but a low state of grace compared to being "filled with all the fulness of God."

The regenerate state is a blessed one, and includes a great and precious work in the soul. An entirely sanctified state is a still greater and more glorious one; but even this may be regarded as *comparatively* not a very high state of religious attainment.

49. *Is there not danger of putting the standard of holiness too high?*

Not if we keep to the Scriptures. The Bible standard of duty and privilege is given so plainly and in such a variety of ways, he that runneth may read, and none need mistake it. See II Corinthians 7:1; I John 1:7, and 3:3; I Peter 1:15; Ephesians 1:4; I Thessalonians 5:23. The apostle says, "Love is the fulfilling of the law"; hence, "The end [the substance and fulfillment] of the commandment is love out of a pure heart." The Saviour gave the standard very plainly as follows: "Thou shalt love the Lord thy God with all thy heart, and with all thy mind, and with all thy strength, and thy neighbor as thyself." There is more danger of putting it lower, than higher than this.

SECTION VII

51. *Will you present some evidences that holiness is attainable?*

The Bible plainly teaches:

1. That God commands us to be holy. "Thou shalt love the Lord thy God with all thy heart, and with all thy soul, and with all thy strength, and with all thy mind and thy neighbour as thyself" (Luke 10:27). "Be ye *holy,* for I am holy" (I Peter 1:16). "Be ye therefore *perfect,* even as your father which is in heaven is perfect" (Matt. 5:48).

2. We are expressly *exhorted* to be holy. "Having, therefore, these promises, dearly beloved, let us cleanse ourselves from all filthiness of the flesh and spirit, perfecting holiness in the fear of God" (II Cor. 7:1).

3. It is expressly *promised* in the Scriptures. "Then will I sprinkle clean water upon you, and ye shall be *clean:* from all your *filthiness,* and from *all your idols,* will I *cleanse* you" (Ezek. 36:25). "Blessed are they which do hunger and thirst after *righteousness* [holiness]; for they shall be *filled*" (Matt. 5:6).

4. That entire sanctification is attainable is evident from the fact that the *commands* and the *promises* stand *correlated* to each other. What God commands, he promises to aid us in doing. If he commands us to love Him with all our heart, He promises, "The Lord thy God will *circumcise thy heart,* and the heart of thy seed, to love the Lord thy God with *all thy heart,* and with *all thy soul*" (Deut. 30:6). If he commands us to "be holy,"

36

he promises, "From *all your filthiness,* and from *all your idols* will I *cleanse you*" (Ezek. 36:25).

5. The possibility of attaining this state is seen in the *declarations* of Scripture. "Jesus Christ is made unto us wisdom, and righteousness, and *sanctification,* and redemption" (I Cor. 1:30). "And that ye put on the new man, which after God is created in righteousness and *true holiness*" (Eph. 4:24). "To the end that he may *establish* your hearts *unblamable in holiness* before God" (I Thess. 3:13). "For God hath not called us unto *uncleanness,* but unto *holiness*" (I Thess. 4:7). If these, with kindred declarations, are true, *holiness* is *attainable.* If they are not true, the Bible is not true.

6. Christ and the apostles *prayed* for it. *"Sanctify* them through thy truth" (John 17:17). "Thy kingdom come; thy will be done in earth as it is in heaven; *deliver* us from *evil*" (Matt. 6:10). "Create in me a *clean heart,* O God; and renew a right spirit within me" (Psalm 51: 10). "And the very God of peace *sanctify you wholly;* and I pray God your whole *spirit,* and *soul,* and *body,* be preserved *blameless* unto the coming of our Lord Jesus Christ" (I Thess. 5:23). Inspired men made holiness the subject of *definite, fervent,* and *earnest prayer.*

7. It is the grand *object* of an established ministry. "And he gave some, apostles; and some, prophets; and some, evangelists; and some, pastors and teachers; for the *perfecting* of the *saints,* for the work of the ministry, for the edifying of the body of Christ, till we all come in the unity of the faith, and of the knowledge of the Son of God, unto a *perfect man,* unto the measure of the stature of the *fullness of Christ*" (Eph. 4:11).

If it has respect to the *priesthood* of Christ, it is "Wherefore he is able also to save them to the uttermost." Is it a state *described?* It is, "Blessed are the pure in heart." Is depravity represented as deep and indelible as scarlet

and crimson? It is, "They shall be as white as snow."
Does it present a *Divine Prototype*? It is, "As he [Christ]
is, so are we in this world." Does it present the *instru-
mental* cause? It is "Sanctify them through thy truth."
Does it present the *meritorious* cause? It is, "The blood
of Jesus Christ his Son," who "gave himself a ransom
for all." Is human agency involved in the work? It is,
"He purifieth himself, even as he is pure." Is the proximate *conditional* cause stated? It is, "Sanctified by faith
that is in me," and, "Purifying their hearts by faith." Is
the grand *efficient agent* referred to? It is, "Through
sanctification of the Spirit." Is the *time stated*? It is,
"Behold, now is the accepted time," and, "Come, for all
things are now ready." Does it declare *who shall enter
heaven?* It is, "He that hath clean hands and a pure
heart."

That holiness is attainable is clear from the fact that
it is represented in the Bible as *having been experienced.*
Suggestive in this line are the accounts of: Enoch (Gen.
5:24); Noah (Gen. 6:9); Job (Job 1:1); Abraham (Gen.
17:1); Asa (I Kings 15:11); Isaiah (Isa. 6); Zacharias
(Luke 1:6).

St. John says: "Herein is our love *made perfect";* and,
"Hereby we know that we dwell in him, and he in us."
St. Paul says: "Ye are my witnesses and God also, how
holily, and *justly,* and *unblamably* we behaved ourselves
among you." St. Paul appeals to the Church, and to
God himself, to witness to the truth of his profession.
To be *holy, just,* and *unblamable,* is to be entirely sanc-
tified. See Luke 1:6; I Thessalonians 2:10; I John 4:17.

52. *If entire sanctification is attainable, why do so few
experience it?*

There are a variety of reasons, the same as there are
a variety of reasons why more sinners are not converted.
The main reason in both cases is an unwillingness to

come to Christ and comply with his conditions. This question can be answered by asking, If conversion is attainable, why are so few converted? If any are *converted*, more might be; and if any are *entirely sanctified*, others may be.

1. It is not that God is unwilling. "This is the will of God, even your sanctification."

2. Nor is it that some are born more depraved than others. "He is able to save them to the uttermost, that come unto the Father by him."

3. Nor is it because some have fewer helps and privileges than others. God requires "according to what a man hath, and not according to what a man hath not."

Dr. Lovick Pierce gives his views thus: "The desire of entire sanctification is dying out in the Church, because the grade of religion our people have been running upon is below the level where sanctification begins." —*Sermon before Gen. Con.*

53. *Can a person successfully seek the gradual attainment of entire sanctification?*

No; for the following reasons:

1. He who seeks a gradual sanctification, seeks necessarily something *less* than entire sanctification; that is, he does not seek entire sanctification at all.

2. He who does not aim at the extirpation of all sin from his heart *now*, tolerates some sin in his heart *now*. But he who tolerates sin in his heart is not in a condition to offer acceptable prayer to God. "If I regard iniquity in my heart, the Lord will not hear me."

3. Inbred sin (the destruction or removal of which constitutes entire sanctification) is a *unit*, a *simple evil principle*, and cannot be *divided* or *subdivided* and removed in parts.

54. *Does the Scripture imagery employed to illustrate the work of entire sanctification imply rapidity and dispatch?*

It does. The imagery employed is that of death by mortification, death by crucifixion, the refining of metals, working of leaven, creation, ablution, the cleansing of the leper, e. g., "Mortify therefore your members which are upon the earth" (Col. 3:5). "Knowing this, that our old man is crucified with him, that the body of sin might be destroyed" (Rom. 6:6). *"Create* in me a clean heart, O God" (Psalm 51:10). "Which after [the image of] God is *created* in righteousness and true holiness" (Eph. 4:24). "Purge me with hyssop, and I shall be clean" (Psalm 51). Leprosy was incurable by human means, was cured only by a *special work of God,* and was effected in a moment. The cleansing of the leper was an emblem of the removal of sin. The whole process was short. Christ said: "I will, be thou clean, and immediately his leprosy was cleansed" (Matt. 8:3). Again, "I will turn my hand upon thee, and purely purge away thy dross, and take away all thy tin" (Isa. 1:25). "And he shall sit as a refiner and a purifier of silver" (Mal. 3:3). This is another short process.

55. *Is it not objected that the terms "corruption," "defilement," and the like, are too physical to be asserted of the soul?*

It is; and is a result of efforts to be wise "above what is written." These terms are given in the Bible; they are very numerous, are in both Testaments, and are more used than any others. The philosophy of human depravity God has not revealed. The fact He reveals and amply illustrates, and uses the figures in question to do it.

The Bible clearly teaches, that the soul in its fallen, unsaved state is *"diseased," "defiled,"* and *"polluted,"* and needs *"washing," "purging," "cleansing,"* and *"healing."* It is both scriptural and reasonable to believe that human depravity is a corrupt, diseased condition of soul, analogous to a diseased, polluted human body. The predisposing evil tendency in the heart is the exponent of an *underlying, radical evil,* or corrupt nature.

56. *Can a state of entire sanctification be secured by ordinary growth in grace?*

It cannot; for the following reasons:

1. Growth in grace is neither a *destroying,* nor a *washing,* nor a *crucifying,* nor a *cleansing* process. Entire sanctification is a death, a washing, a purification. "The blood of Jesus Christ his Son cleanseth us from all sin."

2. Growth in grace has respect to *addition,* to *enlargement* and *development,* and belongs entirely to the positive in Christian life—the graces of the spirit. Growth is an increase or development of some living force: not a *destroyer* or *transformer* of any living force.

3. Growth in grace is a *natural process,* involving culture and discipline, and appertains to spiritual life. Sanctification is a *supernatural* and divine work wrought in the soul. Growth, the *natural, gradual* process of development, should not be mixed with the *instantaneous, supernatural* work of purgation and purification.

4. In growth in grace, the soul is *active* and *co-operative.* Entire sanctification is something *experienced,* and not something *done.*

5. *Growth* never changes the *nature* of any thing; hence, a believer cannot *grow pure,* for the same reason that a sinner cannot grow into a saint—growth not changing the nature of things. A pure nature may grow, and an impure one may grow, and mere growth does not change the one or the other.

57. *In what sense is entire sanctification instantaneous?*

1. If, by entire sanctification be intended the act of cleansing the justified believer from *inbred sin,* it is instantaneous in the same sense as regeneration. Not necessarily in the "twinkling of an eye," at least so far as our perceptions are concerned, but is a *short, quick, rapid* work, the same as the new birth. It is instantaneous as a *death* or a *birth,* as a *washing* or *refining.* Note the imagery—(question 54).

2. The *preparatory process* is usually more or less gradual; hence, Bishop Hamline says: "It is *gradually approached, but instantaneously bestowed."* Before regeneration, there was a gradual process of conviction, repentance, humiliation, consecration, and faith; but they did not regenerate the soul in *part,* or in *whole,* they preceded it. Preceding entire sanctification there is a gradual process of obtaining light, receiving conviction, hungering after purity, confession, prayer, and faith. These do not gradually sanctify the soul, but precede that work.

58. *If growth in grace does not cleanse the heart, what does it accomplish?*

It secures a progressive Christian life. Growth is an essential condition of life, and all development of life is by growth. The life of righteousness, embracing all the features of Christian character, gathers *strength, symmetry,* and *stature* by development.

Growth in grace is so related to the soul's *activities* and *voluntary powers* and the formation of its habitudes, as to secure increasing spiritual strength and moral vigor; hence, it will secure easier and more complete victories over inbred sin.

59. *Is there a distinction between purity and maturity?*

There is, and a very important one. Identifying and confounding these lie at the base of nearly every objection made to an instantaneous sanctification; and has occasioned many strange notions, and much confusion upon this subject.

1. *Purity* has respect to moral *cleanness* or freedom from the defilement of sin. "Wash me, and I shall be whiter than snow." Health is not manhood. *Maturity* has respect to moral *stature* and *strength*—to *adulthood*. "The fullness of the measure of the stature of Christ."

2. *Purity,* in the light of gospel provisions, is a present privilege and duty. "Be ye holy." *Maturity* is a question of *time,* and is subject to the laws of growth and development. "Grow in grace."

3. *Purity* being *instantaneous,* may be received at once. "Believe on the Lord Jesus Christ, and thou shalt be saved." *Maturity* is a gradual, progressive, and indefinite development. "Take heed, and add to your faith virtue."

Maturity is nowhere made a condition of entrance into heaven, while purity is.

60. *What is the voice of the leading writers on sanctification in respect to its instantaneousness?*

They teach that the work of entire sanctification proper —the cleansing of the heart by the Holy Spirit—is instantaneous. Those who teach otherwise, invariably confound *purity* with *maturity,* and predicate a gradual sanctification upon the growth and maturity of the Christian virtues.

The following quotations will be seen to agree with our positions on this subject:

Wesley: "As to manner, I believe this perfection is *always* wrought in the soul by a *simple act of faith;* consequently *in an instant.*" He further says: "Look for it every day, every hour, every moment. Why not this hour —this moment? Certainly you may look for it now, if you believe it is by faith. And by this token you may

surely know whether you seek it by faith or by works.—
Sermons, Vol. I, p. 391.

Adam Clarke: "We are to come to God for an instantaneous and complete purification from all sin, as for instantaneous pardon. In no part of the Scriptures are we directed to seek the remission of sins *seriatim*—one now and another then, and so on. Neither in any part are we directed to seek holiness by gradation. *Neither a gradation pardon nor a gradation* PURIFICATION *exists in the Bible.*"—*Theology,* p. 208.

Nathan Bangs says: "Those who teach that we are *gradually to grow into a state of sanctification,* without ever experiencing an *instantaneous* change from *inbred sin to holiness*—are to be repudiated as *unsound—antiscriptural* and *anti-Wesley.*"—Article in Guide, 1854.

Richard Watson: "To this faith shall the promises of entire sanctification be given, which in the nature of the case, supposes an instantaneous work immediately following upon entire and unwavering faith."—*Institutes,* Vol. II, p. 455.

Rev. J. S. Inskip says: "I apprehended in all cases where any special success has been given to the teaching of this doctrine, it has been where the instantaneous character of the work has been made very prominent."—*Method of Promoting Perfect Love.*

61. *Will you give some evidence that entire sanctification is instantaneous?*

Purity being *God's work,* and being *by faith,* is evidence that it is instantaneous, the same as its kindred blessings—pardon, adoption, and regeneration.

The commands, exhortations, and promises of the Bible teach that *purity* is instantaneous. God desires, commands, and expects instant obedience. This cannot be done if holiness is not instantaneous. God *commands,*

"Be ye holy," plainly requires present holiness; "Be ye filled with the Spirit," "Be ye therefore perfect," enjoins perfection today. "This is the will of God, even your sanctification," means *now*.

The fact that inborn sin is a *unit*, an evil *principle* or taint infecting our nature, and cannot be removed by parts, any more than its antagonism, the principle of life in Christ can be imparted gradually in our regeneration, is evidence that sanctification is instantaneous.

The uniform experience of all who are clear in the light of personal holiness teaches that purification is instantaneous and not gradual. Experience has but one voice on this subject, that is, that it was sought by consecration and faith, and received the same as regeneration, by direct divine power.

62. *Do not some enjoy Christian purity who did not seek it instantaneously?*

Undoubtedly this is the case. A large class of Christians, and some entire denominations, whose Christian character we do not question, do not believe in sudden conversions, and yet there was a definite moment when every one of them who is a Christian was pardoned and regenerated, and his new life began. They were neither pardoned nor regenerated gradually. Many who believe in sudden conversions cannot tell the precise time of their conversion. They know they are converted, and can say, "Whereas I was blind, now I see," but cannot tell the time of the change. The same holds true in regard to entire sanctification.

63. *Is the seventh chapter of Romans a portrayal of Christian experience?*

It is not. As this is quoted so often to prove the necessary existence of sin in the Christian believer, we will quote Dr. Steele:

"This (the 7th of Romans) was never designed to depict the ideal Christian life, but is rather the portrayal of the struggles of a convicted sinner seeking justification by the works of the law."—*Dr. Steele: Love Enthroned,* p. 79.

SECTION VIII

64. *Is this doctrine and experience susceptible of experimental demonstration?*

It is. The essential facts of personal salvation are *knowable*—they may be known by *experience*. The fallen condition of man with all his deplorable convictions, sufferings, and degradation, is not more a matter of assurance, and positive consciousness, than their counterpart in the redemption of Christ—*pardon, adoption, regeneration,* and *sanctification.* The latter come as clearly and fully within the purview of experimental knowledge as the former. We believe with Lord Bacon, that *experience should be the test of truth";* and with Dr. C. H. Fowler, "Entire sanctification will, sooner or later, afford the best solution of any difficulties we may have on this subject."

There are three things that are distinct in this experience:

1. There is a consciousness of inbred sin and moral deficiency after conversion, and the more devoted and faithful the justified soul, the clearer and stronger this conviction.

2. There is conviction, in the light of gospel provisions, of the duty and privilege of being "cleansed from all sin," and made "pure in heart."

3. It is prayerfully sought and *experienced* as an instantaneous cleansing by faith in the blood of Christ.

65. *What is the first direction you would give to a person seeking holiness?*

47

Endeavor to obtain a correct and distinct view of the
blessing promised and needed. What is it? The exter-
mination of indwelling sin—carnal nature from the soul.
It is such a destruction or removal of inbred sin, as to
make the heart—the *fountain* of thought, affection, desire, and impulse—pure.

66. *What is the second direction you would give?*

Come to a *firm* and *decided* resolution to seek until
you obtain a pure heart. It will require a resolution
which will not cower when the knife is put to the heart
to amputate its idols. Your purpose must be *settled,*
decided, uncompromising, and *unconquerable.* None but
an invincible resolution will answer. "The day of the
Lord is near in the *valley of decision.*"

67. *What is the third direction you would give?*

Humble yourself under the hand of the Almighty.
Spiritual *poverty* is the prelude to spiritual enlargement.
"*Blessed are the poor in spirit.*" Do not seek too easy
a way. Be willing to die to sin. Endeavor to feel the
deep, malignant, hateful nature of your depravity, and
your need of purity.

68. *What is the fourth direction you would give?*

Make an *entire consecration* of yourself to God—your
soul, body, time, talents, influence, and *your all*—a complete assignment of *all* to Christ. Search and surrender,
and re-search and surrender again, until you get every
vestige of self upon the altar of consecration. There is
no sanctification without *entire consecration.*

69. *What is the proximate condition of sanctification?*

Faith. "Believe on the Lord Jesus Christ, and thou
shalt be saved." Faith is the immediate condition of sanctification, and God always saves the moment true faith
is exercised. You ask, "Believe what?"

1. *Believe* that God has *promised* it in the Holy Scriptures.

2. *Believe* what God hath promised He is *able* to perform.

3. *Believe* that He is *able* and *willing* to do it now.

4. *Believe that He doth it.*

70. *What degree of faith is necessary to entire sanctification?*

No degree. *Faith* is necessary. Sanctification is by faith. "Believe on the Lord Jesus Christ and thou shalt be saved." Sanctification requires no *greater degree* of faith than justification. Faith, in the two instances, does not necessarily differ in *degree,* but in the *object* for which it is exercised. The idea that faith for entire sanctification, and faith for pardon, differ in degree, has no foundation in either Scripture or reason.

71. *Is saving faith conditional?*

It is. Faith, or confidence in God, cannot coexist with voluntary transgression; the one will destroy the other. "If our heart condemn us not, then have we confidence toward God." The condition is that of *heart approval.* "If our heart condemn us not." Our heart approves us when we wholly submit to God. At this point we can have "confidence toward God." "Confidence in God" is a necessary sequence of heart approval.

72. *What is the chief hindrance to the exercise of saving faith, when the heart has submitted to God?*

Being governed by our feelings, or a desire to possess the *fruits* of faith before we *believe.* We want to go by *sense* and *feel* first. Many are more solicitous about *feeling* than faith. We want to see signs and wonders before we believe. We have no right to expect feeling, the *fruit* of faith, before we believe. We might just as well want to taste our food before we eat it. It will never do to make a saviour of our feelings. Many persons spend their time in vain efforts to force themselves into a right state of feeling. Feelings do not result from a direct effort to feel, but from true faith.

The soul must *repose* on the fullness and efficacy of the atoning blood. It is leaning *there, singly, exclusively* there, that brings the cleansing power. True faith takes the promise, and rests on the infinite merit upon which the promise is based.

73. *Why is it that many who desire holiness, read, and pray, and resolve, and weep, and struggle, yet make but little progress?*

It is mainly because they refuse to comply with the conditions on which the blessing is suspended. One man sees that if he would be holy he must adopt a new system of benevolence. Another sees, as he approaches the clear light of perfect love, a probable call to the ministry, should he go forward. Another sees a large class of duties, hitherto neglected, which must be performed. No man can be entirely sanctified while his body is an "instrument of unrighteousness" in any sense, privately or publicly. God never does for any one what he can do for himself. The putting away of all "filthiness of the flesh" is a part of entire sanctification which every one must perform for himself.

74. *In what sense is faith the gift of God?*

God gives *truth*, the *object* of faith, and the ground of faith, and the *power* to believe; but he believes for no one. While he *helps* the *believer*, the *act* of *believing* is purely the believer's, and is *voluntary*.

75. *In what sense does faith involve a voluntary exercise of the mind?*

In *attention, assent,* and *submission.* First, we are voluntary in giving proper *attention* to the truth, with its evidences; secondly, we are, in a measure, voluntary in giving *assent* and *credence* to apprehended truth; thirdly, we are voluntary in the *practical reception* of the truth, and in *submission* to its claims, which involve *trust* and *reliance*.

76. *Will you give John Wesley's views of the faith that sanctifies?*

"But what is that faith whereby we are sanctified, saved from sin and perfected in love? This faith is a divine evidence or conviction—

"1. That God hath *promised* this sanctification in the Holy Scriptures.

"2. It is a divine evidence or conviction that what God hath promised He is *able* to perform.

"3. It is a divine evidence or conviction that he is *able* and *willing* to do it *now*.

"4. To this confidence that God is *able* and *willing* to sanctify us *now*, there needs to be added one thing more —a divine evidence or conviction that he *doth* it."— *Sermons*, Vol. I, p. 390.

77. *What is meant by simple, naked faith?*

By a *simple* faith is meant, taking God at his word without doubting or REASONING; and by *naked* faith is meant, faith independent of *all feeling*, and *stripped of every other dependence but* CHRIST ALONE.

78. *May I come to Christ now, just as I am?*

Yes, precious soul, this very moment. May the Lord help you! You can make yourself *no better*. We cannot save ourselves in *part* before coming to Christ. *Tears, groanings, resolutions*, and *lamentations* will make us no better, nor more worthy. *"Now* is the day of salvation"; *now* is the time you should believe. It is wrong not to believe. Say, Here, Lord, I *will,* I *do* believe; thou hast said *now; now* let it be. And *now* rest your soul on the all-atoning merit of Jesus.

79. *How may we know that our consecration is unreserved or entire?*

We may be as certain that we have devoted every thing to God of which we have present knowledge, as we are of any mental operation. A *knowledge* of what we possess is all we can give, as it is all our will commands, or over which it has power. We must *know* something of a thing before we can will anything in reference to it. If we consecrate everything of which *we have knowledge*, we meet the gracious requirements of God's law, and reach the full measure of our obligation. If increasing light shall reveal more, the consecration already made covers it, and we have only to lay it on God's altar.

80. *How may we know our consecration is accepted?*

This may be known by the positive word of God, by the witness of the Spirit, by the divine response to faith, and by self-evident intuition.

1. What God says, *we know*. His word of promise is, *"I will receive you."* Can anything be more positive?

2. In the light of the *"witness of the Spirit,"* we know it, just as we know that the sun shines when he is pouring his mid-day beams upon the world. "We have not received the spirit of the world, but that which is of God, that we *may know* the things freely given to us of God."

81. *In what attitude toward God does entire consecration place the soul?*

In the attitude of an *obedient spirit*. In personal consecration to God, there is the vital principle, or germ of all obedience. Obedience is not so much in the *outward act* as in the *state* of the will. This is reasonable and scriptural. Submission, or consecration, has respect to the will, and is manifested in exterior action, and external action is the outcome of the *interior principle* of obedience. Hence all true obedience has prior existence in the human heart, *in an obedient spirit.*

Christ said, "This is the love of God, that ye keep his commandments"; and, "Love is the fulfilling of the law." Love to God is not a mere transient emotion, but a state of *will* and *affection,* and is inseparable from genuine faith. *"Faith which works by love and purifies the heart."* Let it ever be remembered, that *love to God* is an abiding, general preference of the will, or a state of will underlying our whole moral activity, and determines all its particular acts to the one end of obeying and pleasing God. Love in the entirely sanctified soul becomes a *disposition,* or *character.*

82. *Is there a distinction between entire consecration and entire sanctification?*

There is; and the *act* of entire consecration should not be confounded with the *fact* of entire sanctification. Submission to God, or entire consecration, *is our act,* with assisting grace. Entire sanctification *is God's work,* wrought in the soul. Sanctification follows consecration in point of time, as the offering is made before the sin-consuming power is received. Sanctification always includes consecration; but entire consecration does not necessarily include entire sanctification—it *precedes* and *accompanies it.*

83. *What is the difference between the consecration previous to conversion and that previous to entire sanctification?*

They are essentially the same, each involving submission to God and the true spirit of obedience. But, while in principle they are the same, that which precedes entire sanctification is made with a *fuller and deeper sense* of the import of full submission to God. The *penitent,* seeking *pardon,* consecrates himself to the full extent of his discovery of truth and duty; but only with the light of a convicted sinner. The *believer*, seeking *purity*, renews this consecration, in view of the revelations which increasing light, time, and the word of God have made of his duty and moral defiency.

84. *Is any particular standard of conviction necessary in seeking holiness?*

To believe in the doctrine of sanctification, and at the same time to know that you have not experienced it, and need it, is all that is necessary. Certainly, this is all that is necessary to commence seeking it; then, if deeper convictions are needful, they will be given in the improvement of present convictions. The object of *conviction* is to lead to *action*. "Knowledge is conviction"; and a clear perception of duty is all that a *rational* being should ask.

85. *Is the process of receiving full salvation the same in all cases?*

It is essentially the same: submission and faith. All is consecrated, and faith in Christ is exercised. In all cases there must be a practical recognition of divine authority, by unreserved submission to God, and appropriating faith in the merit and power of Christ. These are absolutely necessary to being sanctified wholly, body, soul, and spirit.

The links in the chain of God's order in human salvation are: 1st, *conviction;* 2nd, *submission;* 3rd, *faith;* 4th, the *work of the Spirit.* This order must be seen to be natural, reasonable, and scriptural. If one of these links be wanting, the work must be defective. We may not always note these different steps, yet they are taken in every genuine sanctification.

86. *Is any certain amount of feeling or emotion necessary in seeking purity?*

The Bible presents no particular standard of *feeling* to which all must come. Our temperaments will have much to do with our feelings. It is not necessary that all should have the same amount of feeling, in order to seek either *justification* or *sanctification.* All must be brought, not to the same degree of *emotion,* but to entire *submission* to God, to the terms of salvation, and the consequences that may follow.

87. *Do deep convictions for holiness sometimes obscure, for the time, the light of present justification?*

Doubtless this is often the case. It commonly happens that a Christian earnestly seeking full salvation, comes to the conclusion that he really has much less grace than he thought he had. Sometimes the person seeking holiness will cast his confidence away altogether, and conclude he was deceived, and had never been born again. This is an error, and should be carefully guarded against. It is often the case that such find so much sin remaining in them, and the corruptions of their hearts, by being restrained and opposed, becomes so chafed and apparent, that they do not perceive the evidence of the grace they have received.

88. *Are the convictions of the sinner seeking pardon, and of the believer seeking entire holiness, the same?*

They differ materially. The penitent sinner is convicted of *guilt,* of *condemnation,* of the divine displeasure, and his need of pardon. Those of the believer seeking purity, are convictions of *inward depravity, unlikeness to God,* and his need of *cleansing.* They produce *pain* and *shame,* but not condemnation.

89. *What are the fruits of conviction for the blessing of regeneration?*

A renunciation of sin; a confession of sin; an honest regret for sin; a turning from the vanities of the world;

a resolute seeking of God; a strong anxiety to do his will, and pray for pardon and salvation.

90. *What are the fruits of conviction for the blessing of perfect love?*

Deep self-abasement and humility of spirit; self-renunciation and submission to God; self-loathings, and hungerings and thirstings after righteousness; and a willingness to suffer any thing, be any thing, or do any thing to please God and obtain a pure heart.

91. *What are the usual exercises of mind in seeking holiness?*

They are directly the reverse of what many suppose. The process is a *humbling, sifting, searching, crucifying* one. When the believer begins to pray for holiness, instead of receiving at once a baptism of sweet heavenly fire and glory, the soul begins to see more and more of its own *vileness, deformity,* and inward *corruption.* God makes to the soul a more clear and painful discovery of remaining *impurity.* The soul has no more depravity now than it had before, but is becoming more thoroughly acquainted with itself. It has now a clearer view of the tendency in itself to evil, and of the fact that it is shut up to the grace of God for help. Hence it is that, when a believer begins to pray for purity, he appears to himself to *grow worse and worse.* This spiritual poverty and crucifixion is sometimes very distressing, but in the nature of the case, is a necessary process. At this point there is much danger of getting discouraged, and giving up; here many fail at the very threshold of success. "*Blessed* are they that *mourn,* for they shall be *comfort-*ed." "Blessed are the *poor* in *spirit,* for theirs is the kingdom of heaven."

92. *In seeking holiness, is it important that prayer should be definite and discriminating?*

All indefiniteness is in the way of seeking purity. We seldom get *special* blessings by *indefinite* prayers.

We have ample authority for definiteness in prayer. David, who longed for inward purity, prayed, "Create in me a *clean* heart, O God." The Saviour prayed, *"Sanctify* them through thy truth." The Apostle prays, "The very God of peace *sanctify* you wholly," These are specific prayers for the blessing of entire sanctification. Why should you not ask for the very blessing you need and desire? Why pray at *random*? When you want one thing of your fellow-men, you do not ask for another, nor for every thing.

93. *Should a clear evidence of justification precede the seeking of entire sanctification?*

This should usually be the case; but there may be exceptions, as in those persons who have lost their justification by *refusing* to *seek holiness.* We think such persons, in some instances, may regain the light of justification in connection with their entire sanctification. But God's usual order is, first the *light of justification,* and then the *work of entire sanctification.*

Many, we fear, who commence seeking entire sanctification in a *backslidden state,* on being blessed, conclude they are in the possession of perfect love, when in fact, they are only reclaimed backsliders. Such often bring reproach upon the cause of holiness. It is very desirable to start in the clear light of regeneration and justification to seek for the Canaan of perfect love.

94. *Will you give your views of Mark 11:24? "What things soever ye desire when ye pray, believe that ye receive them, and ye shall have them."*

We do not presume this passage to teach that any blessing can be received *independently* of the *established conditions* of its bestowment; that *faith* in the *fact* of receiving a blessing is the *condition* of receiving it. Such faith would involve the absurdity of believing it is *done* and it *will be done.*

The faith that *saves,* that *claims* the promise, that *relies on God's word,* must precede the consciousness or interior witness of possession. There can be no room for *saving faith* after visible or tangible manifestations, or after the blessing is received. It is a matter of knowledge then.

SECTION IX

THE EVIDENCES OF PERFECT LOVE

95. *What is the character of the evidence of a state of entire sanctification?*

It is just as *strong, positive,* and *reliable* as can be given to substantiate any fact. Indeed it is the very strongest of all evidence.

1. The testimony of *consciousness.* This testimony we can no more doubt than we can doubt our existence. No testimony is more certain than this. By it we *know* we live and breathe, love or hate, sit or stand, or walk, and that we are joyful or sorrowful, happy or wretched.

2. The testimony of God—"The witness of the Spirit." This testimony is *divine, direct,* and *positive.* The Holy Ghost is the *witnessing* Spirit.

96. *Did Mr. Wesley teach that we may have the same evidence that we are sanctified that we have that we are justified?*

To the question, "But how do you know that you are sanctified, saved from your inbred corruption?" Mr. Wesley replies: "I can know it no otherwise than I know that I am justified. 'Hereby know we that we are of God,' in either sense, 'by the Spirit that he hath given us.' We know it by the witness and by the fruit of the Spirit."—*Plain Account*, p. 118.

97. *Ought any one to believe that he is sanctified wholly before he has the witness of the Spirit?*

Mr. Wesley says: "None, therefore, ought to believe that the work is done till there is added the testimony of the Spirit witnessing his entire sanctification *as clearly as his justification.*"—*Plain Account*, p. 79.

This position of Mr. Wesley is safe, and applicable as a general rule; and yet, perhaps, there may be some exceptions to it, as in those cases where God may be pleased to hold the soul for a season, after the work is done, to a *naked* faith in His word, before the Spirit's witness is given. If we do not mistake, this has been the experience of some of the clearest witnesses of perfect love. Perhaps the same may be true in some cases of justification.

98. *What is the witness of the Spirit?*

It is a sweet, inward persuasion of the Spirit, that God, for Christ's sake, has either pardoned my sins and regenerated my soul, or that the blood of Jesus Christ has cleansed it from all sin.

99. *Is the witness of the Spirit to regeneration and to entire sanctification different?*

They differ only in the facts to which the Spirit gives his testimony in the two cases. In the one case, it is a delightful and decisive persuasion that God has pardoned our sins and converted our souls. In the other, it is a delightful and decisive persuasion that the blood of Jesus Christ cleanseth us from all sin.

100. *Is the evidence of sanctification, or the witness of the Spirit, always clear at first?*

"Indeed, the witness of sanctification is not always clear at first, (as neither is that of justification;) neither is it afterward always the same, but, like that of justification, sometimes stronger and sometimes fainter. Yea, and sometimes it is withdrawn. Yet, in general, the *latter testimony* of the *Spirit* is both as *clear* and as *steady* as the former."—*Plain Account,* p. 119.

101. *Is it our privilege to possess the witness of the Spirit without any intermission?*

"Some have the testimony both of their justification and sanctification, without any intermission at all, which,

I presume, more might have, *did they walk humbly* and *closely with God.*"—*Wesley's "Plain Account,"* p. 122.

102. *Is true evangelical faith usually accompanied with the witness of the Spirit?*

It is. When real faith is exercised, and the work of entire sanctification fully wrought, the witness of the Spirit may be expected, and it is usually *apprehended then with greater or less distinctness.*

103. *Can the witness of the Spirit be retained while any sin is committed or allowed?*

Mr. Wesley says: "It is inevitably destroyed, not only by the *commission* of any outward sin, or the *omission* of any known duty, but by giving way to any *inward sin;* in a word, by whatever *grieves* the Holy Spirit of God."—*Sermons,* Vol. I, p. 94.

104. *Are there certain fruits which necessarily flow from a pure heart as evidence of holiness?*

The experience carries much of its evidence with it, so that the saved know it. They feel it, they confess it, and they diffuse it abroad in the *sweetness* of their spirit, and in the *purity of their lives.*

105. *By what fruit of the Spirit may we know that our hearts are cleansed from all sin?*

"By love, joy, peace, always abiding; by invariable long-suffering, patience, resignation; by gentleness, triumphing over all provocation; by goodness, mildness, sweetness, tenderness of spirit; by fidelity, simplicity, godly sincerity; by meekness, calmness, and evenness of spirit."—*Plain Account,* p. 94.

106. *What are the fruits of inbred sin, and how does it manifest itself in the heart?*

The fruits of inbred sin are pride, anger, self-will, jealousy, covetousness, peevishness, impatience, hatred, variance, emulations, strife, envyings, unbelief, and such like. These do not *reign* in the justified believer, but keep up more or less of a warfare within the soul; "the flesh lusteth against the Spirit, and the Spirit against the flesh; and these are contrary the one to the other." Inbred sin manifests itself to the consciousness of the partially sanctified by clinging to the appetites and tendencies of the soul, and seeking and struggling for unlawful indulgence. Hence the risings of anger, pride, self-will.

107. *Is the emotional experience in the moment of sanctification various?*

There is doubtless as great a variety as in justification and regeneration. Some are exercised in one way, some in another; some have one class of emotions, and some another. Sometimes there is an *unusual illumination* of soul. Sometimes a *sweet resting and sinking into Christ.* Sometimes great *joy* and *ecstasy,* though this is not the general experience. Sometimes there is an astonishing *increase of faith,* and *assurance that all sin is gone.* Sometimes an overwhelming sense of the *divine presence.*

108. *Will Christian perfection make all persons act just alike, and appear to equal advantage?*

Christian perfection removes all sin, and makes the soul perfect in love; but it is no part of its office to destroy *personal distinctions* or *innocent peculiarities.* It will give a good, sincere, pure heart; and, other circumstances being equal, it will invariably impart, in all respects, real and manifest superiority. In the *essentials* of Christian character it will make any man superior to what he was without it.

109. *Will a state of entire sanctification clearly evidence itself by the absence of all sin?*

It will; and *any* sin, whether of *motive,* of *will,* of the *desires,* or of the *life,* negatives its existence. Men may know as surely that they are in a *sanctified state* as that they are in an *unsanctified state,* and may know it in the *same way*—by consciousness and by the testimony of

God. Those who are *pure* in heart, and filled with the Holy Spirit, obey God *decidedly, constantly, unhesitatingly, unreservedly, cheerfully,* and *easily:* to such the will of God is supreme—the end of all controversy. The question of obedience is never raised, but is settled.

110. *Will entire sanctification enable me to pray, believe, and rejoice every moment, even in the severest trials?*

It will, doubtless, so far as it is naturally, or perhaps I should say *physically*, possible. While the soul may have seasons of heaviness, sore conflicts, and protracted trials, which are often very necessary, it may still possess a heaven of peace, and love, and light in its ocean depths. This enables the sanctified soul to pray, and believe, and rejoice, every moment, or to "rejoice evermore, pray without ceasing, and in every thing give thanks."

> "I worship thee, sweet will of God
> And all thy ways adore,
> And every day I live, I seem
> To love thee more and more."

111. *Are deep grief and sorrow of soul incompatible with perfect love?*

Mrs. Hester Ann Rogers says: "Satan suggested I ought not to have felt any grief; but the Lord teaches me I may *feel grief very sensibly* and *keenly*, consistent with *pure love* and *entire resignation*."

The purest of men are sometimes in *heaviness* of spirit; they often wade through deep waters of affliction; sometimes they pass through fiery trials from *sickness,* or *poverty,* or from the *bereavement* of friends, and they may be grieved, depressed, and afflicted; but they are not without grace, and comfort in the Holy Ghost. The quiet of their spirit is untouched, and they are never destitute of peace.

112. *What is the rest which the sanctified soul enjoys?*

The Saviour says, "My peace I give unto you." "The work of righteousness [holiness] shall be peace, and the effect of righteousness quietness and assurance for ever."

It is a state of sweet rest from all conflict between the will and the conscience. "The body of sin has been destroyed," and the soul has peace with itself—inward quietude. "It will feast your souls with such peace and joy in God (says Wesley) as will blot out the remembrance of everything that we called peace or joy before."

> "Now rest, my long-divided heart;
> Fixed on this blissful center, rest;
> Nor ever from thy Lord depart—
> With him of every good possessed."

113. *What are the natural and necessary indications of a pure heart?*

A pure heart differs vitally from an impure one in the fact that its *expressions* of *goodness* are natural and spontaneous, the fruit of a gracious nature, and not *unnatural* and *forced.*

The Saviour says, "Ye shall know them by their fruits." The streams partake of the nature of the fountain. The heart gives character to the life by a law of necessity. It breathes itself through all our activities, and a pure heart will be indicated by reluctance to mingle with the *gay,* the *vain,* and the *worldly.* It has no moral affinity for such society, and no taste for such associations. The charm of the world has been broken. The pure heart has tastes, motives, communings, and enjoyments totally dissimilar to the worldling.

114. *Is it not very difficult to retain the clear light of full salvation?*

We answer, No. It is less difficult than to retain the continuous light of justification and neglect full salvation. In order to retain justification, we have to live *obediently,* and that can be done more easily with a pure heart than with an impure one. All things considered, the *easiest* religious life is the fullest and least obstructed religious life. A little religion is more difficult to retain than a heart full. Full salvation includes *clear* light, a *submissive* will, *strong* faith, *nearness* to God, *intense* spiritual affinities, *worldly* charms broken, and *healthful* activities, all of which combine in making the religious life *natural* and *easy by the grace of God.*

115. *Does entire sanctification secure the "full assurance of faith"?*

It does; and as we believe, the only grounds for "the full assurance of faith." It cuts the knots of doubt and uncertainty, and makes the evidences of Christian experience strong, and the path of duty plain.

116. *Is an entirely sanctified state a blissful one?*

In reading the gospels and epistles we are struck with the *joyousness, hope,* and *triumph,* mentioned of believers everywhere. The words which we see most frequently are *"Love," "Joy," "Peace," "Praise," "Thanksgiving," "Joy unspeakable and full of glory."* The primitive church was a "royal priesthood," "a holy nation," going to Mount Zion with songs and triumph; and not a company of *weeping, doubting, fearing, trembling, groaning* professors.

117. *Do the Scriptures authorize a confession of what God does for us?*

They do. David says, "Come and *hear,* all ye that fear God, and I will *declare* what he hath done for my soul." Jesus said to one whom He had healed, "Go home to thy friends, and *tell* them how *great things* the Lord hath done for thee, and had compassion on thee." Paul says, "If thou shalt *confess* with thy *mouth* the Lord Jesus, and shalt believe in thine heart that God hath raised him from the dead, thou shalt be saved. For with the heart man believeth unto righteousnesss [holiness], and with the *mouth confession* is made unto salvation." In his Letter to Timothy, a young minister of the gospel, he says, that he, Timothy, *"professed* a good *profession* before many witnesses." The apostle exhorts the Hebrew brethren after this manner: "Let us hold fast our *profession.*" David says, "Thy saints shall bless thee. *They shall speak of the glory of thy kingdom,* and *talk of thy power,* to make known to the sons of men his mighty acts, and the glorious majesty of his kingdom." Our Saviour repeatedly declared, "Whosoever shall *confess me before men,* him shall the Son of man also confess before the angels of God." No fear of man, nor false modesty, should seal our lips against an honest confession of perfect love.

118. *Does the Bible teach that Christians are God's witnesses?*

It does. "Ye are my *witnesses,* saith the Lord." "Ye shall be *witnesses* unto me, both in Jerusalem, and in all Judea, and in Samaria, and unto the uttermost parts of the earth." Nearly all the Scripture characters gave their testimony to what God did for them—to their experience.

119. *Does the church generally recognize a profession of religion as a duty of believers?*

It does. A profession of reliigon is the acknowledged duty of all true Christians. It is recognized in all branches of the Protestant church. *Believing* with the *heart* and *confessing* with the *mouth,* stand closely connected; and "what God hath joined together," no man has a right to put asunder. The mouth must and will *speak,* when the heart believeth unto righteousness; for "of the *abundance* of the *heart* the *mouth speaketh.*" The *belief* and *experience* of the heart, and the *confession* of the *mouth,* must go together. The *possession* of perfect love, and a desire for its *diffusion,* are inseparable, and this desire *prompts* to a *profession.*

120. *To what is the Christian to give his testimony?*

A witness is to testify to what he *knows.* A Christian is to testify regarding his experience, *"the truth, the whole truth, and nothing but the truth."* Any ambiguity or concealment by a witness, is a high offense against civil statutes, and an insult to any court of justice. Every court in the world would dismiss from the stand as an incompetent witness any one who could only affirm a *belief,* a *desire,* or a *hope* respecting the facts involved in his testimony. He who witnesses for Christ must tell just what he *has done.*

121. *Will not the spirit, conversation, and example exhibit what grace has done, so as to exclude the necessity for a profession?*

These are important and indispensable, but are not the whole of our duty. If the sanctified soul can be excused on this ground from professing holiness, then the converted sinner can be excused on the same ground with equal propriety from any profession, and we should have no professors at all.

122. *Should Christian labor and testimony go together?*

They should. After Pentecost, Peter and John went down to Samaria to labor for Christ, and *"testified and preached* the word of the Lord." Christ declared unto Paul, that He appeared unto him to make him "a *minister* and a *witness."* Here a distinction is made between preaching and witnessing, and that both are essential parts of ministerial duty. Paul often fell back upon his religious experience, and related it as simply and directly as possible, and published his experience to the world with its remarkable details, visions, power, and visit to the third heaven included. He says, "Christ liveth in me"; "I am crucified with Christ"; and, "Ye are my witnesses, and God also, how holily, and justly, and unblamably we behaved ourselves among you."

123. *Does not so rich a grace deserve a humble, faithful, and grateful acknowledgment?*

When the soul is baptized with the Holy Ghost, and sin is utterly destroyed, and love, pure, perfect love, fills the whole heart, there are the most solemn obligations of faithful testimony for God. Rev. William Bramwell wrote to a friend, "Live in purity of heart. Be saved from all sin, and DECLARE *this at* EVERY PROPER SEASON." And yet the vast mass of Christian professors, Bishop Thomson said, "are like the rivers emptying into the Arctic Sea, are frozen over at the mouth."

124. *Can the witness of entire sanctification be retained without confession on suitable occasions?*

It cannot. To retain perfect love requires continued obedience to all the will of God. Not to gratefully acknowledge his grace and work in us, is *disobedience,* and *grieves* his Holy Spirit. The united testimony of those clear in this experience has but one voice on this question.

Rev. William Bramwell says: "I think such a blessing cannot be retained without professing it *at every fit opportunity;* for thus we glorify God, and with the mouth make confession unto salvation."—*Memoir.*

Rev. John Fletcher lost this grace *four* or *five* times by not *declaring it.*

125. *What good will be secured by confessing perfect love?*

A Christian testimony will obey and please God. "Ye are my *witnesses,* saith the Lord."

It will benefit the confessor. This is not questioned in regard to regeneration; why should it be in regard to entire sanctification? Bishop Hamline says, the confession of holiness "promotes humility," "aids self-consecration," and "strengthens faith itself." James Caughey says: "The more frequently I spoke of this great blessing, confessing it, and urging others to press after it, the *clearer* my evidence became." Lady Maxwell says: "I am enabled to bear a more public and decided testimony for Christian perfection by my *lips* and *pen,* and I find that the Lord *owns me in it,* at *least,* so far *as it respects my own soul."*

It will benefit others. "Many shall hear it, and fear and trust in the Lord." This is never doubted in regard to justification, why should it be in regard to our complete cleansing?

126. *Should holiness be professed before a promiscuous audience?*

There should be prudence and judgment exercised in this, as in all other Christian duties. In the confession of "perfect love," the same prudence and judgment should be exercised as in the confession of justification, **as to** time or place. Christ bade his disciples **"cast not** their pearls before swine," intimating a proper discrimination with respect to circumstances and hearers. There may be seasons and occasions when it will be wise and useful to give testimony before all classes. But this profession, the same as that of justification, should usually be made among the pious, and in social meetings.

127. *What terms are best and safest in professing holiness?*

We are always safe in keeping close to the Bible. We may reasonably infer that the Holy Ghost has chosen the best terms expressive of his own work. Bible terms are less likely to mislead people than those of our own selection. While we do not think there is any authority for shutting a man up to any particular form of expression, yet we have no right to ignore the inspired terms significant of this blessing. "Higher life," "life of faith," "more religion," "a deeper work of grace," and like phrases, are well enough in their place, but should not take the place of the deeply significant words of inspiration. God has named His own religion. "And a highway shall be there, and a way, and it *shall be* CALLED, *The way of* HOLINESS; the unclean shall not pass over it." "Why, then," asks Dr. Adam Clarke, "are there so many, even among sincere and godly ministers and people, who are so much opposed to the *terms*, and so much alarmed at the *professor?*

128. *Should the profession be definite, and in terms which will not mislead?*

It should. We should not be so indefinite, or make choice of such terms as amount to an actual or virtual denial of the work, or a refusal to bear the responsibility of this "high and holy calling." It is the truth that we are to profess, the exact truth, in our experience.

129. *Do not some profess this experience in terms seriously objectionable?*

Very likely; as there is no Christian duty that has not been abused by inconsiderate, rash, and weak minds. The same is true in the profession of justification. It cannot be expected that the profession of holiness will be wholly free from exhibitions of human frailty. The world is full of *uncultivated, careless, rash, inconsiderate,* and *impetuous* men, and the profession of holiness, like all other Christian duties, is liable to abuse from them. Unwise *professions* of holiness, however, argue no more against its profession, than the *abuse* of *prayer* argues against the duty of *prayer.*

130. *Is not the profession of holiness, assumed by some, as of itself evidence of spiritual pride?*

Rev. Charles G. Finney says: "It seems next to impossible, with the present views of the church, that an individual should really attain to this state, and profess to live without known sin, in a manner so humble as not of course to be suspected of enormous spiritual pride. This consideration has been a snare to some who have hesitated, and even neglected to declare what God had done for their souls, lest they should be accused of spiritual pride. And this has been a serious injury to their piety."—*Letter to Preachers.*

131. *Does not the profession of perfect love as a distinct blessing tend to produce jealousy and discord among brethren?*

It does not among *Christians.* A confession of entire sanctification in suitable words, in a proper manner and place, and in the right spirit, will produce no jealousy or discord among *real* Christians. It may among a class of backsliders, and dead or doubtful professors.

John Wesley says: "Nor does any thing under heaven more quicken the *desires* of those who are justified, than to converse with those whom they believe to have *experienced a still higher salvation.*"—Vol. VI, p. 502.

132. *Did Mr. Wesley encourage the profession of Perfect Love?*

He did. Note the following quotations from his journal and letters.

"One reason why those who are saved from sin should freely *declare it* to believers is, because nothing is a stronger incitement to them to seek after the same blessing."

"You *can never speak too strongly or explicitly* upon the head of Christian perfection. If you speak only *faintly* and *indirectly*, none will be offended and none profited."

"It requires a great degree of watchfulness to retain the perfect love of God; and *one great means of retaining it, is frankly to declare what God has given you,* and earnestly to exhort *all the believers you meet with to follow after full salvation."*—Vol. II, p. 13.

"By silence he might avoid many *crosses* which will naturally and necessarily ensue if he *simply declare,* even among believers, what God has wrought in his soul. If, therefore, such a one were to *confer* with *flesh* and *blood,* he would be *entirely silent.* But this *could not be done with a clear conscience,* for undoubtedly he ought to speak."—Vol. VI, p. 502.

He writes to his brother Charles, who was about to visit Macclesfield, where there were a large number of witnesses of holiness: "I believe you will rather encourage them to *speak humbly* and *modestly,* the words of truth and soberness. Let your knowledge *direct,* not *quench, the fire. That has been done too much already."* See Vol. II, p. 130-133.

133. *Did Mr. Wesley profess Christian perfection?*

He did. Any minister who speaks of entire sanctification as Mr. Wesley did, is regarded as a professor of holiness. He says:

"You have over and over denied instantaneous sanctification to me; but *I have known* and taught it above these twenty years."—Vol. IV, p. 140.

"Many years since, I saw that without holiness no man shall see the Lord. I began by following after it and inciting all with whom I had any intercourse to do the same. Ten years after, God gave me a clearer view than I had before of the way how to attain it, namely, by faith in the Son of God. And immediately *I declared* to all, '*We are saved from sin, we are made holy by faith.*' This *I testified in private,* in *public,* in *print,* and God confirmed it by *a thousand witnesses.*"—Vol. VII, p. 38.

Those who say Mr. Wesley did not profess perfect love, do so because he does not, as they claim, state it in his Journals. We admit Mr. Wesley seldom recorded his *personal religious experience* in his Journals, and yet we have as much regarding his experience of sanctification as of justification.

134. *Did Mr. Wesley find opposition in the church to the profession of holiness?*

He did. Happy would it have been for the church of God, if every Methodist minister had followed the advice of the great founder of Methodism. But, alas! how many, instead of laboring to help and protect those who have professed Christian holiness, have sided with their opposers, and labored to put down the profession of holiness in the church! If the apostles and martyrs had only held their peace, kept quiet, and *lived their religion* only, they might have saved their heads.

It is not strange that Satan should oppose Christian testimony, for St. John says this great accuser of the brethren is overcome "by the blood of the Lamb, and by the *word of their testimony.*"

135. *Is there not a want of harmony in Mr. Wesley's teaching on this subject at successive periods?*

There is, between his early and abandoned views, and his mature and established views.

Mr. Wesley's mind underwent some changes concerning Christian perfection during his early ministry. He had occasion to modify some expressions, and change his opinions somewhat several times before he became fully established in the doctrine. There was a great revival of holiness about 1760, and we have no reason to believe that his views changed at all after that time. He died in 1791.

136. *Were the experience and profession of holiness common in the early days of Methodism?*

They were. We have records of *professions of perfect love* in *all* the journals of the old Methodists. They all speak of *witnesses* of *regeneration,* and also of *sanctification.* Indeed, the golden pot of Methodist biography is brimful of the *manna* of *sanctified experience.*

"In London alone I found *six hundred and fifty-two* members of our society who were exceedingly clear in their experience, and whose *testimony* I could see no reason to doubt."—*Wesley's Sermons,* Vol. II, p. 223.

Bishop Asbury says: "I think we ought modestly to tell what we feel *to the fullest.* For two years past, amidst innumerable trials, I have enjoyed almost *inexpressible sensations.* Our *Pentecost* is come in some places for *sanctification.* I have good reason to believe that upon the eastern shore *four thousand* have been converted since the first of May last, and ONE THOUSAND SANCTIFIED."—*Journal.*

137. *Is there not danger of professing this blessing when it is not possessed?*

There may be some danger of it, but not any more, if as much, as there is in regard to justification. We think there is more danger of not acknowledging all that God does for us, than of professing more than he has really wrought in us. Better a few mistakes than *universal silence*.

138. *At what points is caution necessary in the profession of perfect love?*

1. It may be professed too soon, before it is really attained. It may be confessed with too little humility of manner. All carelessness should be avoided in the profession of holiness.

It may be done with too much self-confidence, or with self-seeking. It may be done with too much reliance upon the mere profession as a means of retaining holiness. The soul should never rest for salvation on any thing itself has done or may do, instead of resting on Christ

SECTION XI

WITNESSES OF PERFECT LOVE

139. *Will you give some testimonies from those who have enjoyed perfect love?*

We give a few brief extracts from many thousands who have confessed this grace; these are selected from the various Christian denominations of this country and Europe, and are scattered through two or three centuries.

1. Rev. John Fletcher: "I will *confess* him to *all* the *world;* and I declare unto you, in the presence of God, the *holy Trinity,* I am now 'dead indeed unto sin,' and alive unto God. He is my *Prophet, Priest,* and *King;* my indwelling holiness; *my all in all."—Journal of H. A. Rogers,* p. 136.

2. Bishop Hamline: "All at once, I felt as though a hand not feeble, but omnipotent, not of wrath, but of love, were laid on my brow. I felt it not only outwardly, but inwardly. It seemed to press upon my whole body, and *to diffuse all through and through it a holy, sin-consuming energy.* As it passed downward, my heart as well as my head was conscious of the presence of this soul-cleansing energy, under the influences of which I fell to the floor, and, in the joyful surprise of the moment, cried out in a loud voice. . . . For a few minutes, the deep of God's love swallowed me up; all its waves and billows rolled over me."—*Guide to Holiness,* 1855.

3. Dr. Thomas C. Upham: "I was distinctly conscious when I reached it. . . . I was then redeemed by a mighty power, and *filled with the blessing of perfect love."* . . . "I was never able before that time to say, with sincerity **and** confidence, that I loved my heavenly Father with

76

all my strength. But, aided by divine grace, I have been enabled to use this language, which involves, as I understand it, the true idea of Christian perfection or holiness, both then and ever since."—*Guide to Holiness*. Professor Upham was a Congregationalist.

4. Rev. James B. Taylor, Presbyterian: "I am ready to *testify* to the *world,* that the Lord has blessed my soul beyond my highest expectations. People may call this blessing by what name they please—'faith of assurance,' 'holiness,' 'perfect love,' 'sanctification.' It makes no difference with me whether they give it a name or no name; it contains a blessed reality, and, thanks to my heavenly Father, it is my privilege to enjoy it; it is yours also, and the privilege of all, to enjoy the same, and to go beyond any thing that I have ever yet experienced." . . . "Some, I expect, are a little disaffected to think I *profess the doctrine of perfect love.* They do not understand, because they *have not experienced it.*"

5. Dr. Sheridan Baker: "Now the way of faith opened to my spiritual vision with such clearness that I definitely made the reckoning and unequivocally declared the fact. This was followed immediately by a flooding of love and heavenly sweetness, which I have no language to describe. I was now fully persuaded of my entire sanctification. The attitude of my soul is now that of complete, unreserved, and eternal surrender to God. . . . Just now I feel, with almost unendurable sweetness, the bliss of the purified. Hallelujah!"—*Divine Life*, March, 1879.

6. Mrs. Phœbe Palmer: "I rejoiced in the assurance that *I was wholly sanctified* throughout *body, soul,* and *spirit*. Oh, with what triumph did my soul expatiate on the infinitude of the atonement. I saw its unbounded efficacy as sufficient to cleanse a world of sinners, and present them faultless before the throne. I felt that I was

enabled to *plunge* and *lose myself in this ocean of purity:*
yes,

> 'Plunged in the Godhead's deepest sea,
> And lost in love's immensity.' "

7. Bishop R. S. Foster: "Here again the Spirit seemed
to lead me into the inmost sanctuary of my soul—into
those chambers where I had before discovered such defilement, and showed me that all was cleansed, that the
corruptions which had given me such distress were dead
—taken away, that not one of them remained. I felt the
truth of the witness; it was so; I was conscious of it, as
conscious as I ever had been of my conversion. . . . What
a wonderful deliverance the Lord has wrought. Ought
not I to praise Him? Ought not I to publish this great
salvation? What a rest He hath found for my soul! A
rest of naked, simple faith. To him be glory for ever.
Amen."—*Guide*, 1850.

8. Madam Guyon:

> "A little bird am I,
>   Shut from the fields of air,
> And in my cage I sit and sing
>   To him who placed me there—
> Well pleased a prisoner to be,
> Because, my God, it pleaseth Thee.
>
> "Naught have I else to do;
>   I sing the whole day long;
> And He whom most I love to please
>   Doth listen to my song.
> He caught and bound my wandering wing,
> And still He bends to hear me sing.
>
> "My cage confines me round;
>   Abroad I cannot fly;
> But though my wing is closely bound,

My heart's at liberty.
My prison walls cannot control
The flight, the freedom of the soul.

"Oh! it is good to soar,
    These bolts and bars above,
To Him whose purpose I adore,
    Whose providence I love,
And in thy might will I find
The joy, the freedom of the mind."

Madam Guyon was clear in this experience, receiving it by faith; and for professing and teaching justification and sanctification, was imprisoned in the French Bastille for four years. While in prison she penned the beautiful lines we have given. So deep and blissful was her religious experience, she declared: *"The very stones of my prison appear like rubies in my eyes."*

9. Dr. Adam Clarke: "I regarded nothing, not even life itself, in comparison of having my heart *cleansed from all sin;* and began to seek it with full purpose of heart." . . . "Soon after this, while earnestly wrestling with the Lord in prayer, and endeavoring self-desperately to believe, *I found a change wrought in my soul,* which I endeavored, through grace, to maintain amid the grievous temptations and accusations of the subtle foe."—*From a letter to John Wesley.*

10. Dr. Edward Payson, Congregationalist: "Were I to adopt the figurative language of Bunyan, I might date this letter from the land of Beulah, of which I have been for some weeks a happy resident. The Sun of righteousness has been gradually drawing nearer and nearer, appearing larger and brighter as he approached, and now he fills the whole hemisphere, pouring forth a flood of glory, in which I seem to float like an insect in the beams of the sun, exulting, yet almost trembling, while I gaze

upon this excessive brightness, and wondering with unutterable wonder why God should deign thus to shine upon a sinful worm."—*Encyclopedia of R. Knowledge.*

11. Rev. William Bramwell: "My soul was all *wonder, love,* and *praise.* It is now about twenty-six years ago; *I have walked in this liberty ever since.* Glory be to God! I have been kept by His power. By faith I stand. . . . I then *declared to the people* what God had done for my soul; and *I have done so on every proper occasion since that time, believing it to be a duty.*"—*Life of Bramwell.*

12. Dr. Daniel Steele: "Suddenly I became conscious of a mysterious power exerting itself upon my sensibilities. My physical sensations, though not of a nervous temperament, in good health, alone, and calm, were like those of electric sparks passing through my bosom with slight but painless shocks, melting my hard heart into a fiery stream of love. Christ became so unspeakably precious, that I instantly dropped all earthly good—reputation, property, friends, family, everything, in the twinkling of an eye; and my soul cried out:

'None but Christ to me be given,
None but Christ in earth or heaven.'"
Advocate of Holiness, 1870.

13. Dr. E. M. Levy, Baptist: "I seemed filled with all the fullness of God. I wept for joy. All night long I wept. All the next day, at the family altar, in the street, and in the sanctuary, tears continued to flow. The fountain of my being seemed broken up, and my heart was dissolved in gratitude and praise. My soul seemed filled with pulses, every one thrilling and throbbing with such waves of love and rapture that I thought I must die from excess of life."—*Advocate of Holiness,* 1872.

14. Mrs. Edwards, wife of the famous Jonathan Edwards: "In the house of God, so conscious was I of the joyful presence of the Holy Spirit, that I could *scarcely*

refrain from *leaping with transports of joy.* My soul was *filled* and *overwhelmed* with *light,* and *love,* and *joy* in the Holy Ghost, and seemed just ready to go away from the body. . . . This exaltation of soul subsided into a *heavenly calm* and a *rest* of soul *in God,* which was even sweeter than what preceded it."

"A cloud of witnesses," of living, intelligent, competent "witnesses," have testified to their own happy experience of perfect love; and what is all the negative experience in the universe compared to this?

SECTION XII

REASONS WHY EVERY CHRISTIAN SHOULD BE ENTIRELY SANCTIFIED

140. *Why should every Christian possess perfect love?*

1. Because, without it, we can neither *do,* nor *be* all that God commands. His greatest, and much repeated command is, "Thou shalt love the Lord thy God with all thy heart, and with all thy soul, and with all thy mind." We certainly cannot love God with *all* our heart, while indwelling sin remains in it. He commands us to "rejoice evermore," to "love our enemies," to "pray without ceasing, and in everything give thanks," to "reckon ourselves dead indeed unto sin," to "be clothed with humility," to "be filled with the spirit," and to "be holy," all of which is impossible without a pure heart.

2. Because without entire sanctification it is impossible to be *free from indwelling sin,* the rudiments of the "carnal mind," which is enmity against God. These disturbing, discordant elements—"roots of bitterness"—will spring up and trouble us. The death of the "old man," the "body of sin," by *crucifixion, mortification,* or *destruction,* is imperative. It is commanded: "Mortify, therefore, your members, which are upon the earth." "That our old man is crucified with him, that the body of sin might be destroyed."

3. Because, without it, the remaining evils of our unsanctified hearts will often *prevail* in our passions and propensities, and our Christian characters will be marred and defective. While any forces remain in the heart, antagonistic to grace, the Christian is not fully prepared for the *conflicts* and *race* before him.

4. Because, if our hearts are not *cleansed* from *inbred sin,* the work of grace will be so *interrupted* and *obstructed* by it, that we cannot become "*rooted and grounded in love.*" No man can become *thoroughly settled and established,* like a tree whose roots strike deep and extend without obstruction in every direction, while his heart remains uncleansed.

5. Because, without Christian purity our growth in grace will be *obstructed and unsteady.* Christian purity secures the best possible ground for rapid growth in love, knowledge, and power.

6. Because, without entire sanctification our knowledge of personal salvation is necessarily *superficial,* as we *know only in part.* Without an experimental knowledge, we cannot know personally that "The blood of Jesus Christ his Son cleanseth us from all sin." Some things can be known only by experience.

7. Because, without holiness we cannot be free *from distressing convictions of moral deficiency*—that we are not what we ought to be, in view of the *possibilities and necessities* of the Christian life.

8. Because, without purity our communion with God will inevitably be *intermittent.* None but the pure in heart are free from the disturbing antagonisms of grace. Inbred sin interrupts communion with God. It is only the pure in heart who have constant fellowship with the Father, the Son, and the Holy Ghost.

9. Because, without perfect love we cannot be entirely saved from *tormenting, slavish, unsanctified fear.* "Perfect love [alone] casteth out fear"; and he that is not in possession of this grace has some "fear that hath torment." "God is love; and he that dwelleth in love dwelleth in God, and God in him. Herein is our love made perfect, that we may have boldness in the day of judg-

ment. There is no fear in love. *He that feareth is not made perfect in love.*"

10. Because, without perfect love we cannot enter fully *into gospel rest,* and possess undisturbed peace of mind. Purity alone can secure soul rest—freedom from all the disquieting and jarring discords of indwelling sin. "We, which have believed, do enter into rest."

11. Because, *purity* is essential to *"full assurance of faith,"* and a *continuous* witness of justification. Inbred sin darkens our spiritual vision, often obscures the clear light of justification, and is fruitful of *darkness, doubts,* and *fears.* Conscious confidence in Christ and a conscious neglect of privilege and duty cannot coexist in our hearts.

12. Because it is the end and aim of the whole Christian system. Holiness is the grand object and aim of the gospel economy. For this purpose Christ died, the Holy Scriptures were given, the means of grace instituted, and the work and agency of the Holy Ghost furnished "And *holiness* without which no man shall see the Lord."

13. Because, if not sought there is the utmost danger of backsliding. Not to go forward is to go back, and *"end in the flesh."* There is no standing still in a religious life. Israel could not stay on the borders of the promised land; they had either to go over, or measure their steps back into the wilderness.

14. Because, without entire sanctification we cannot occupy the *best vantage-ground* to resist temptation and achieve complete victory over Satan. Holiness involves all the elements of stability and strength, and affords power in the hour of trial, and great moral endurance in the conflicts of life. It secures *the safest possible condition of probation.* "Be strong in the Lord and in the power of His might. Put on the whole armor of God,

that we may be able to stand against the wiles of the devil."

15. Because, without perfect love we cannot possess that full measure of *religious joy* and healthful happiness which God has provided for us, and which our nature and circumstances require. The enjoyments of the entirely sanctified heart are *full, purely religious,* and *divine.*

16. Because, without entire sanctification we cannot reach the *maximum* of our spiritual power, or attain our greatest usefulness. Other circumstances being equal, God always graduates the Christian's influence by his purity. *Love and purity* are the strongest elements of moral power, and he who has them is invincible.

17. Because, perfect love is the most pleasing *expression* of *gratitude* to God for His infinite goodness. When we were in our sins, he convicted, pardoned, and regenerated our unworthy soul. Should we not be as entire now in the service of God as we were in the service of the devil? We are under infinite obligations of love and praise to God. He has given us his *Son*, his *Truth*, and his *Spirit*. He has provided for us a *seat in heaven,* a *robe of righteousness,* a *harp of gold,* a *crown of glory,* and a *special place in the center of his eternal love.* "That where I am there ye may be also."

18. Because, God is holy—*essentially, absolutely, unchangeably,* and *transcendently* HOLY. He is the infinite *model* and *source* of holiness, and desires that all his creatures should be holy. Because it is written, "Be ye yourselves also holy."

19. Because, holiness has *intrinsic excellence* and *glory* in itself. It brings a whole *constellation of virtues* into a single heart—perfect love, perfect faith, perfect humility, perfect patience, and perfect purity. Here are riches

and honors, like the source whence they emanate, glorious as heaven and lasting as eternity.

20. Because, the interest of the Redeemer's kingdom demands it. We cannot glorify God fully without it. The lives of Christians are to be the practical exponents of the holy principles of Christ's spiritual kingdom. "Ye are the light of the world." Millions of sinners are perishing for want of holy ministry and membership. Of Barnabas it is written: "He was a good man, and full of the Holy Ghost and of faith; and much people were added unto the Lord."

141. *Is not death a sanctifier?*

It would seem that many believe so. This may not be said in words, but actions speak louder than words. The greater part of believers defer their sanctification until death, while death itself has no more to do with the believer's *sanctification* than with his *justification.*

1. The Bible nowhere states or intimates that *death sanctifies* the soul.

2. While the sacred writers speak often of the *means,* the *agencies,* and the *time* of sanctification, they never name death as its means, its agent, or its time.

3. If death sanctifies the soul, then it, at least, is partially our Saviour; and thus the *effect* of sin (for "death is by sin") becomes the means of finally destroying it.

4. If sanctification, as the Bible teaches, involves *human agency,* the *free, intelligent action* of the mind, "sanctified by faith," "through the truth," death is no process of cleansing the soul.

5. If death sanctifies the soul, then the work is removed from the ground of moral agency, and we have no responsibility in the matter. This would nullify all the precepts requiring our agency to obtain personal holiness.

6. The change produced by death is in our physical state and mode of being, and a mere physical change of state cannot relieve the soul of its pride, unbelief, selfishness, and corrupt lusts. Change of character is God's work, and is by grace, through faith, by moral means.

7. Many appear to believe the old pagan dogma that the body is the seat of sin, and that depravity pertains only to the body, and that when the body dies, as the soul leaves the body it will be free from depravity; but Christian sanctification has less regard to the body than to the soul, which is the seat of inbred sin. The carnal mind, or *selfishness,* pride, anger, covetousness, impatience, hatred, and all filthiness of the spirit, belong to the *soul* and not to the *body.*

142. *If none are saved without entire sanctification, what becomes of those who deny this doctrine?*

The "pure in heart" alone "shall see God." Before men leave this world they must be purified and made perfectly holy, or they can have no place in the kingdom of God. God has no two sets of conditions for believers; all are to be cleansed from all sin by the blood of Christ, either *before* or *at death.*

All justified souls are God's children, are heirs of eternal life, and have a title to heaven, and cannot fail of their inheritance if they do not forfeit their justification by apostasy. All men will be saved who die in a justified state before God, as all such are children of God by *adoption,* are absolved from the guilt of *actual sin* by *pardon,* and are free from any *voluntary* antagonism to holiness. Sudden death to such finds them covered with the covenant of grace, similar to the dying infant, which entitles them to the merits of Christ and heaven.

Although many Christians seem to deny this doctrine, they do, in fact, admit it virtually, if devoted to God. All true Christians have longings after it, and in different phraseology allow in substance what we claim for the entirely sanctified. Some, we believe, in all the several denominations have obtained what we claim as holiness. All believers who are faithful unto death, so trust in Christ and renounce self that he makes them perfect in love and takes them home to heaven. They might have experienced it many years before, and lived as well as died in its possession, had they been properly instructed. Thousands of believers would obtain perfect love if ministers more generally understood the doctrine, enjoyed the experience, and faithfully preached and lived it themselves.

143. *What course do most professors of religion pursue in regard to holiness?*

Like the ancient Israelites, instead of going directly to Canaan, they take a zigzag course of wandering in the wilderness. Their unbelief and disobedience prevent their entering the spiritual Canaan, and subject them to the necessity of a return to Egypt, or to ceaseless wanderings in the wilderness, almost in sight of the beautiful hills of that land, which flows with milk and honey.

144. What are the results of this course on the part of *the Church?*

The results are similar to those which befell the ancient Israelites. The ten *cowardly, unbelieving, rebellious* spies were struck dead on the spot. And may the Lord have mercy on those ministers, who, following the example of the ten unbelieving spies, bring up an evil report from the land. Even some ministers who have been through the land, and have tasted of its precious fruits, have gone back into the wilderness, and have ceased to urge the people to go over. It is to be feared, when Jesus comes, such ministers will be found wanting.

SECTION XIII

MINISTERS SHOULD BE ENTIRELY SANCTIFIED

145. *Is it not vastly important that ministers of Christ be entirely sanctified to God?*

It is. Holiness is the chief element of efficiency in the ministry. Talents, learning, and eloquence without it are "as sounding brass and a tinkling cymbal." Without it the minister can neither live, nor preach, nor labor as he should. There is a *clearness,* a *strength,* a *fullness,* an *energy,* and an *unction* needed in the sacred office impossible without entire holiness.

After the disciples received their great commission, they were *repeatedly commanded* to tarry in the city of Jerusalem until they received *power from on high.* Although they had been under the immediate tuition of the *Master* himself (which was better than any theological school in the world), yet they were not prepared for their work without *"the promise of the Father"—the endowment of power.* "Perfect love casteth out fear," and ministers need it in order to be faithful to all classes, saints or sinners, in or out of the church of God.

Rev. Charles G. Finney says: "To me it seems very manifest that the great difference in ministers, in regard to their spiritual influence and usefulness, does not lie so much in their literary and scientific attainments as in the measure of the Holy Ghost which they enjoy.

"A thousand times as much stress ought to be laid upon this part of a thorough preparation for the minstry as has been. Until it is felt, acknowledged, and proclaimed upon the housetops, rung through our halls of science, and sounded forth in our theological seminaries, that this is altogether an indispensable part of the preparation for the work of the ministry, we talk in vain and at random when we talk of the necessity of a thorough preparation and course of training."—*Letter in Oberlin Evangelist.*

146. *Can a minister successfully preach perfect love without the experience himself?*

He cannot *as clearly,* nor as *successfully* as with the experience. He may, and should preach it, as well as he can, while he may not be clear in the experience; he may present the theory correctly, and may lead some to its enjoyment, but not as he might with the light and power of the grace in his own soul. Christ said: *"The shepherd goeth before the flock, and leadeth them."* How can we expect to send the people ahead of us?

President Mahan writes: "I must myself be led by the Great Shepherd into the 'green pastures, and beside the still waters,' before I could lead the flock of God into the same blissful regions."

"Whatever is our level in Christian life," says Dr. Lovick Pierce, "will be the level of our general membership."

Dr. George Peck says: "How important is a holy ministry! Well was the injunction given, *'Be ye clean that bear the vessels of the Lord!'* The church will scarcely take a higher stand in religion than that which is occupied by the ministry."—*Christian Perfection,* p. 422.

147. *Why is there so little preaching upon this subject?*

Undoubtedly it is because so few of the ministry enjoy it themselves.

Bishop Peck says: "But there are reasons why holiness is not more faithfully preached. It is hard to raise the *stream* higher than the *fountain.* It is hard to preach what we have never experienced, and the fear of the reproach,

'Physician, heal thyself,' we doubt not, hinders many of us from charging home upon the members of the churches their remaining corruptions, their neglect of 'the blood' that 'cleanseth from all sin,' and their exposure to apostasy and final ruin in consequence."

SECTION XIV

HOLINESS MUST BE PREACHED

148. *Should the doctrine, experience, and practice of Christian Holiness be preached frequently?*

This subject should receive (as it demands) great prominence in all our ministerial labors. While it should not be the *only topic* in our pulpit ministrations, it should be a *prominent one*. The Apostle Paul states the great object of an established Christian ministry to be *"for the perfecting of the saints."* In regard to his own labors, he says: "We warn every man, and teach every man, . . . that we may present every man *perfect* in Christ Jesus." The minister of Christ should give the doctrine and practice of holiness the same prominence the Bible gives it.

Rev. John Wesley says: "Therefore let *all* our preachers make a point to *preach* perfection to believers *constantly, strongly, explicitly.*" . . . "*I doubt not we are not explicit enough in speaking on full sanctification, either in public or private.*"—Vol. VI, p. 529.

"I am afraid Christian perfection will be forgotten. Encourage Richard Blackwell and Mr. Colley to *speak plainly.* A general faintness in this respect has fallen on the whole kingdom. Sometimes I seem almost weary of *striving* against the *stream* of both *preachers* and *people.*"

"I hope he is not ashamed to preach full salvation, receivable now, by faith. This is the word which God will always bless, and which the devil peculiarly hates; therefore, he is constantly stirring up both his own children and the weak children of God, against it."—*Letter to Mrs. Bennis,* 1771.

Dr. Adam Clarke says: "Let all those who retain the apostolic doctrine, that the blood of Christ cleanseth from all sin in this life, *press every believer* to go on to perfection, and expect to be saved, while here below, into the fullness of the blessing of the gospel of Christ." —*Theology*, p. 201.

Bishop Asbury: "Night comes on, and I will close with saying, '*Preach sanctification, directly and indirectly, in every sermon.*'" He wrote to another, "O purity! O Christian perfection! O sanctification! It is heaven below to feel all sin removed. *Preach it*, whether they will hear or forbear. PREACH IT."

149. *Did Mr. Wesley preach often upon the subject of holiness?*

We think he did, and for the following reasons:

Mr. Wesley was a consistent man. He says, in his *Plain Account*, p. 88: "If I were convinced that none in England had attained what has been so clearly and strongly preached by such *a number of preachers, in so many* places, and for so long a time, I should be clearly convinced that we had all mistaken the meaning of those Scriptures."

In the journals of Dr. Adam Clarke, Bramwell, Carvosso, Mrs. Hester Ann Rogers, and Lady Maxwell, where a great number of Mr. Wesley's sermons and texts are noticed, you will find a large proportion of them are on the subject of full salvation or perfection. More than one-half of the hymns composed by Mr. Wesley were upon the subject of holiness. The sermons which he published were designed to present a general survey of Christian theology. Let it be remembered that we have but about one hundred and forty of his sermons; while he preached over seven hundred times a year during his ministry, and in his lifetime over forty-two thousand sermons.

150. *Is there not a serious lack on the part of the ministry in preaching on this subject?*

We are compelled to believe there is much less prominence given to this subject by our ministers than there should be.

Bishop Peck says: "Alas! the truth cannot be denied. The great privilege and duty of present salvation from all sin *is omitted in so large a number of sermons* as to leave many in doubt whether there be any such gospel, and *grievously* to *discourage* and *mislead* those whose spirits pant for full redemption."—*Central Idea*, p. 113.

151. *Is it wise to use the phrase "second blessing"?*

We can see no objection to its use, nor any great demand for its use. It has been in use among Methodists for over a hundred years, as Mr. Wesley and the early Methodists frequently used it. Mr. Wesley writes thus: "It is exceedingly certain that God did give you the *second blessing, properly so called.*" . . . "One found peace, and one found the *second blessing.*"—Vol. VII, p. 45.

Charles Wesley put it into his hymns, and without caviling over it, millions have sung for a century:

> "Give us, Lord, this *second rest.*"
> "Speak the *second time,* be clean."
> "Let me gain that second rest."

Even the Calvinistic Augustus Toplady wrote:

> "Let the water and the blood,
> From thy wounded side which flowed,
> Be of sin the *double cure,*
> *Save from wrath,* and *make me pure.*"

Sin is of two kinds, *wrong acts,* and *wrong states,* as a "transgression of law," and as a *defilement* or "*unrighteousness.*" Salvation has a double or twofold aspect: *pardon* and *purity, justification* and *sanctification.*

"Being justified by faith, we have peace with God." "The blood of Jesus Christ, his Son, cleanseth us from all sin." This towfold blessing runs all through the Scriptures, and is taught by precept, promise, and history. Ancient Israel typified them in crossing the Red Sea, and the Jordan; in leaving Egypt, and in entering Canaan.

152. *Is it wise to make holiness a specialty in the church and in Christian effort?*

It is. The Bible makes it a *specialty.* It is the grand *objective* point of the whole Christian system—the *center* where all the lines of truth meet. The *commands, promises, invitations, exhortations,* and *counsels* all run to this "central idea" of Christianity.

Bishop Foster says: "It is the truth glowing all over, welling all through, revelation; the glorious truth which sparkles and whispers, and sings and shouts in all its history, and biography, and poetry, and prophecy, and precept, and promise, and prayer. The great central truth of the system."—*Christian Purity,* p. 80.

The *expediency* of making it a *specialty* is seen in its importance, and in its essential relation to the whole work of God. (See Section XVI.)

To make it a specialty, or give it prominence, does not involve the neglect of other truths, as many seem to suppose. There can be no true presentation of holiness, without presenting its correlated truths in the Gospel. A moment's thought will show that human depravity, the atonement, the work of the Spirit, faith, obedience, and the conversion of sinners, all stand intimately related to it.

No one excels, except he makes his pursuit, for the time, a specialty. College and seminary professors understand this, for in teaching it is deemed essential. Why should "perfect love," as a specialty, be an exception.

"Love" is declared to be "the fulfilling of the law," and love out of a pure heart the end of the commandment.

153. *Is there any opposition in the ministry to putting this subject in the foreground and giving it prominence?*

There is, and always has been. During a hundred years past, those who has *confessed* and *preached* perfect love, and urged believers partially sanctified to press after "the fullness of the blessing of the gospel of Christ," have *seen* opposition and *suffered* from it.

Dr. John P. Brooks says: "Notoriously, there are ministers not a few, who are the authorized expounders of doctrine in the denominations for which they speak, who steadily and purposely ignore the subject of holiness in their pulpit ministrations. . . . There are pulpits, and many of them, from which holiness is declaimed against; from some of them, misrepresented; from others, berated; from still others, calumniated."—*Address at Holiness Conference.*

154. *Is it not claimed that the opposition is in regard to the measures adopted, rather than to the doctrine or experience?*

It is so claimed to some extent; but those who make objections to the measures adopted almost invariably do not claim to possess perfect love themselves, and manifest no sympathy for *instantaneous* sanctification, or any *special meetings,* or *direct means* for its promotion. They rarely preach upon the subject *specifically,* and when they do, they either labor to fault those who teach and profess this grace, or to throw the whole subject into vague and indefinite generalities. Their treatment of the doctrine and experience is the same as those ministers in churches that reject instantaneous sanctification altogether, and only teach growth and Christian culture. The **results are precisely the same: none are led into the** clear light and experience of perfect love, and whole churches become prejudiced against instantaneous sanctification.

155. *Should we not* ASSUME, *that there is no opposition to the spread of this doctrine and experience?*

We should not. To *assume* that there is no opposition to it, is to assume what *is not true,* and what is very generally known not to be true. "To be forewarned is to be forearmed," and there is an opposition, strong and persistent, that every faithful worker in this regard has to encounter. To refuse to look at difficulties and dangers that environ us is not courage, but folly and cowardice.

We should not unduly magnify this opposition, nor dwell much upon it. We should not give it too much attention, nor attach very much importance to it. We are to work as though there were no opposition, and not talk too much about it, so as to let it hinder us. It is especially important that we do not allow it to engender bitterness in our minds, which is the most dangerous item. This should be carefully guarded against, as the many little annoyances and frictions from this source, are calculated to sour or embitter the spirit of those constantly subject to them.

156. *How is this opposition usually manifested?*

By *misrepresentations, false accusations,* and by *taunts* and *sneers* at those who give it prominence.

There is no doctrine of revealed religion that has suffered more misrepresentation than this blessed doctrine of perfect love. There is rarely an article written against it that states it fairly, or that does not more or less misrepresent the teachings of its special advocates.

The sneers and taunts, *"He is one of the sanctified ones," "He makes a hobby of Holiness,"* and the like, are so common, and so fruitful of evil, as to demand attention.

That some go to an unwarrantable extreme in regard to the subject of Christian holiness, we admit, and it is a source of grief to all the true friends of holiness. Untimely and unintelligent efforts are injurious to any cause. Nevertheless, where there is one thus chargeable in regard to this subject, there are fifty who fail to seek this grace, and live beneath their privilege and duty.

This mode of opposition serves to quiet the convictions of many who are dissatisfied with their spiritual condition, and feel the need of a clean heart. The maddog cry of *hobbyism* has frightened multitudes of timid souls from the pursuit of holiness.

Christian holiness and its friends have sufficient opposition in the depraved hearts of the unconverted, and in those who reject the doctrine altogether, without an ambush fire of this kind from their professed friends.

Dr. Abel Stevens says: "Ministers who *profess* and *preach* holiness have to encounter *suspicion, denunciation, theological* and *ecclesiastical ostracism.*" And he asks, "Is it not time that this thing was not only abandoned, but regarded with *shame* and *penitence?*"

There is a class of temporizing, self-indulgent, tobacco-using men in some of our pulpits, who neither believe in, preach, nor enjoy much religion; these are ready to utter such accusations against any who profess or preach Christian holiness, and these manifest and shameful facts are neither *palliated* nor *concealed* by their stale cry of "Croaker!" against wholly consecrated persons who weep over the desolations of Zion.

157. *Is it not often objected to professors of holiness that they indulge in censoriousness?*

It is, and it always will be, so long as there are so many *worldly, formal, backslidden* professors in the church. No man can successfully wage a campaign against the *formalism* or *deadness* which hides itself under the pretense of *dignity* and *decency* without appearing to be censorious. We do not deny that some may have given an occasion for this objection; but let any Christian, in the ministry or laity, do his whole duty to the church and the world in their present state—let him speak *to* them and *of* them as they *really* are—and he will of course incur the charge of censoriousness. Who suffered more of this than Mr. Wesley?

Rev. Charles G. Finney says: "Entire sanctification implies the doing of all our duty. But to do all our duty we must rebuke sin in high places and in low places. Can this be done with all needed severity without, in many cases, giving offense, and incurring the charge of censoriousness? No, it is impossible; and to maintain the contrary would be to impeach the wisdom and holiness of Jesus Christ himself."

With some people it is a common thing if a brother has not "charity" enough to apologize for sin and cover up the "works of the devil," to charge him with "censoriousness," "sour godliness." There can be no holiness which has no rebuke for sin, or opposition to Satan. Look at the Great Exemplar—the Son of God. The Spirit of God and the spirit of the world can never harmonize; they are perfect antagonisms.

158. *Are there two kinds of holiness among men, one a sweet, loving, peaceful holiness, and the other a fighting one?*

Holiness is the same in *kind* in God, angels, and men. It invariably secures *peace, meekness,* and *love* as *sweet* as *heaven.* But these very elements make men hate the devil, and *oppose sin with all their might.* Perfect love makes its possessor as *meek* as a *lamb* and as *bold* as a *lion.* While it inspires *love* and *gentleness,* it teaches an uncompromising opposition to all unrighteousness. It makes its possessor a *burning, shining, loving, fighting, conquering* soldier of Christ.

They said the meek and lowly Jesus had a devil. John Wesley was accused incessantly, for years, of being *heady, willful, self-conceited, censorious,* and *bigoted.* He could be led by a hair in the right direction, but the combined powers of earth and hell could not move him an inch contrary to his honest convictions of duty.

SECTION XV

HOLINESS IDENTIFIED WITH THE PROMOTION OF THE GENERAL WORK OF GOD

159. *Is the general work of God identified with the preaching and the promotion of holiness?*

It is in every respect. This must be so in the very nature of the case, and it cannot be permanently promoted in any other way. We give the following authorities on this question:

Mr. Wesley says: "I examined the society at Bristol, and was surprised to find fifty members fewer than I left in it last October. One reason is, *Christian perfection* has been *little insisted* on; and wherever this is not done, be the preachers ever so eloquent, there is little increase, either in number or in the grace of the hearers."—*Works,* Vol. IV, p. 220.

"I preached at Bradford, where the people are all alive. Many here have lately experienced the great salvation, and their zeal has been a general blessing. Indeed, this I always observe, *wherever a work of sanctification breaks out, the whole work of God prospers.* Some are convinced of sin, others justified, and all stirred up to greater earnestness for salvation."—Vol. IV, p. 437.

Dr. Olin says: "For nearly the last half century little has been said about it in this country. Now the doctrine is reviving again. *With it will come many blessings— great power and grace.*"

Bishop McKendree said to Summerfield: "Never forget that no doctrine which we have ever preached has been more owned by the Head of the Church; and I doubt not the success of your mission may mainly depend upon your zealously holding forth this great salvation."—*Letter to Summerfield.*

Bishop Soule writes to Rev. Timothy Merritt in 1841: "It should be an occasion of gratitude and joy to the whole 'household of faith' this blessed doctrine of scriptural holiness is reviving in the churches—that Christians and Christian ministers of different denominations are waking up to this great concern."

"The calm voice of history will persistently declare," says Rev. Alexander McLean, "that when from within the denomination, this doctrine and experience was assailed by argument or innuendo; or by its being placed in a light so false as to make it repellent, the spiritual and temporal interests of the church correspondently suffered."—*Address at Holiness Conference.*

SECTION XVI

RESULTS OF NOT SEEKING HOLINESS

160. *What are the results of neglecting to seek holiness?*

It affords fearful advantage to Satan, our great enemy.

He comes to enslave the soul with *fear,* to inflate it with *pride,* to inspire it with the *love of the world,* to inflame its *lusts,* to excite *anger,* to *obscure* the path of duty, and induce *rebellion* against God.

It is the occasion of frequent defeat in spiritual conflicts.

Sinning and repenting, rising and falling, are prominent characteristics of those who refuse to seek the blessing of holiness. How truthfully does this familiar stanza describe the lives of multitudes of converted men:

> "Here I repent and sin again;
> Now I revive, and now am slain—
> Slain with that same unhappy dart
> Which, oh, too often wounds my heart."

Rev. Timothy Merritt says: "If Christians would not backslide, and bring a reproach upon the cause of Christ, they must go on to perfection. There is no medium between going forward and drawing back. As soon as any one *ceases to press forward,* he *declines* in spiritual life." —*Christian Manual.*

Professor Finney says: "No man can be a Christian who does not sincerely desire it, and who does not constantly aim at it. No man is a friend of God who can acquiesce in a state of sin, and who is satisfied and contented that he is not holy as God is holy."

The very conditions upon which a state of justification is retained inevitably lead to Christian purity. The same

103

is true of the conditions of retaining a state of perfect love—they are those by which the soul is to grow and mature in holiness. A violation of the conditions of increase and growth in holiness forfeits the state of holiness itself. The way for a regenerated soul to obtain the blessing of perfect love, is to abide closely by the conditions of retaining his justification. If he does, he will soon, very soon, bathe in the fountain, and come out pure through the blood of the Lamb.

Many good men think the church is sadly backslidden on account of this neglect.

"How many thousands have been slain by harbored inward foes, which have seemed to be harmless! *What a mass of backsliders there are now in the Church,* for the very *reason* that they have been satisfied without going on unto perfection!"—*Central Idea,* p. 315.

A neglect to seek holiness causes a spirit of opposition to holiness.

It is usually the case that persons who have been repeatedly convicted of their need of holiness, and of their duty to seek it, and have refused to do it, or have put forth at times some slight efforts to obtain it, and then relapsed into indifference upon the subject, become its worst enemies.

161. *If I lose the blessing, must I tell others of it?*

Usually this would be very improper. It would weaken the feeble-minded, and stagger those who are seeking. Fly directly to Christ. Take Him again by simple faith as a present Saviour. Cry, Lord, here I am; I repent; I give up all; I am fully thine. Thou art my Saviour; I will, I do believe. You might tell an intimate friend or two; they would help you by their prayers.

SECTION XVII

TRIALS OF THE ENTIRELY SANCTIFIED

162. *Are trials and tribulations peculiar to the Christian life?*

They are. Christianity is an antagonism to this wicked world. It always has been, and always will be. The more deep and thorough our piety, the more we are unlike the world, and the stronger its antagonism to us.

Tribulation, to a faithful soul, is no occasion for doubt or unbelief. "Beloved, think it not strange concerning the fiery trial which is to try you, as though some strange thing had happened unto you."

Our Lord Jesus Christ passed through the white-hot furnace of tribulation, and presents an example for our imitation. He suffered all manner of tribulation, and was tempted in all points like as we are. "He was despised and rejected of men"—was spit upon, and endured all manner of bitter, vile, and cruel treatment. He bore it all meekly—leaving us an example of meekness, endurance, and patience.

88 - Testings

163. *How may a state of entire sactification be retained?*
The conditions of *retaining* perfect love, like the conditions of retaining justification, are the same as those by which it was *obtained;* namely, a *complete submission* of the soul to God, and *simple faith* in Christ for *present* salvation. This submission and faith, graduated by increasing light and grace, must continue through life if perfect love be retained.

Watch over your heart, and keep it "with all diligence." Watch over your *lips,* and be jealous of your tongue, and guard against a light and trifling spirit, by which multitudes have fallen into darkness and ruin. Watch for seasons of prayer and special communion with God. Watch for opportunities of doing and for receiving good. Watch against the allurements of the world, and against everything that is *sensual,* and has a tendency to lull the soul to sleep. Watch against temptations, and resist them in a moment—steadfast in the faith. *"Be sober, be vigilant, because your adversary, the devil, as a roaring lion, walketh about, seeking whom he may devour."*

Always remember, *"Thou, God, seest me!"* You are watched and seen every moment by an eye a million times keener than the eyes of angels—the infinite eye of the all-seeing God. If you knew that a legion of angels were watching you every moment, how careful you would be to act aright! Remember you are always in God's immediate presence. Pray *often,* and then prayer will become a *delight. Stay* with God in prayer—stay until He *melts* you, and then stay when you are melted, and plead with him, and he will answer, and you will be *transformed, renewed,* and *strengthened.*

106

SECTION XIX

OBJECTIONS TO CHRISTIAN HOLINESS

164. *Will you reply to the following objections to entire holiness?*

1. *"If all sin were expelled from the heart, the Christian warfare would cease."*

After all sin is expelled from the heart, we shall have a warfare to KEEP it out. Our blessed Saviour was entirely free from sin, but he had a warfare, and was tempted in all points, like as we are, and yet without sin. "The servant is not above his Lord."

2. *"You teach that men can live without sin."*

St. Paul says: "Awake to righteousness, and sin not." David says: "Stand in awe, and sin not." St. John says: "He that committeth sin is of the devil"; that is, he who *knowingly, voluntarily,* and *habitually* sins, is a child of the devil, and not a Christian.

3. *"If any were entirely sanctified, they would immediately die and go to heaven."*

It is generally believed that this poor, wicked world is suffering for want of *holy men* and *women,* more than any other world to which they can be transferred. If as soon as a man becomes holy he must die and go to heaven, this world is truly in a pitiable condition.

4. *"If a soul is entirely sanctified, it no longer needs the blood of Christ."*

Our Lord says, "I am the vine, ye are the branches"; and, "The branch cannot bear fruit of itself, except it abide in the vine; no more can ye, except ye abide in me." "If a man abide not in me, he is cast forth as a [severed] branch, and is withered."

107

5. *"If a man is entirely sanctified, I cannot see any chance for further improvement."*

In answer to this objection, see question 37.

Dr. D. A. Whedon says: "Heretofore the work of the Spirit has affected the *quality* of the love; henceforth it increases the *quantity*. The love is now pure, and future growth gives more and more pure love—the measure of it will depend upon the soul's capacity."—*N. C. Advocate*, 1862.

6. *"This doctrine leads to pride."*

That cannot be, as *perfect humility* is an *essential* part of it. When it can be shown that health leads to sickness, strength to weakness, light to darkness, wealth to poverty, or virtue to vice, then, in the nature of things, this objection may be true.

7. *"It leads to fanaticism."*

That there have been fanatics who have believed and advocated this doctrine, we admit; but we do not admit that Christian holiness either made them fanatics, or tends to fanaticism.

8. *"It sets aside repentance."*

No, indeed! Perfect Christians have a deeper abhorrence of sin, more pungent conviction of their former depravity and guilt before God, and greater holy shame and grief over their present defects, than any other class of Christians.

OBJECTIONS TO SEEKING PERFECT LOVE

165. *What course do many professors of religion pursue in regard to Christian holiness?*

They pursue much the same course in respect to it, that sinners do in respect to *justification;* they neglect it, and endeavor to justify themselves in so doing by various excuses. Some of the excuses are noticed as follows:

1. *"I am not clear in my views of Christian holiness."*

"If any man will do his will," says Christ, "he shall know of the doctrine."

2. *"I regard entire sanctification a great blessing, too great for me to obtain."*

Unbelievers present this excuse for not seeking religion—"It is a great thing to be a Christian." You tell them the provisions of the gospel are ample, mighty, divine. *Are they?*

3. *"If I attempt to seek holiness, I am fearful I shall fail."*

The Bible encourages no such idea; and that should be the rule of our *faith* and *practice,* and not our *imagination.*

4. *"I have known persons who professed holiness to do things which are wrong, and thereby gave no evidence of holiness."*

Admitting it to be true, is it not a reason why *you* should be entirely sanctified, and so "let your light shine" as to disabuse the minds of men regarding this precious doctrine?

5. *"Some have obtained it and lost it, and I fear I should lose it."*

It takes no more grace to keep men saved than it does to save them; and St. Paul asserts, *"My grace is suffi-cient,"* and God *"is able to make all grace abound toward you."*

6. *"If I seek holiness I shall have to change some items of my business, and give up some of my habits."*

If your business or your habits are wrong, you will have to give them up or lose your soul.

7. *"If I were entirely sanctified, I should be obliged to do many duties from which I now excuse myself."*

If honest in this excuse, you have no reason to regard yourself a Christian. A Christian is a man who *loves* and *obeys* God. What right have you to choose to do a *part* of God's will, and refuse to do *a part?*

8. *"If I obtain holiness, and live a holy life, I shall have enemies."*

All the enemies that a holy life provokes will serve a good purpose in the wisdom and power of God, though no thanks to the devil who brings it about.

9. *"If I were entirely sanctified, lived in that state and confessed it, I would be singular, and be subject to ob-servation and talk."*

Men cannot be *public sinners,* and then become *private saints.* This is what sinners would like, but God has no private saints.

10. *"The inconsistencies of some who have professed holiness have prejudiced my mind against it."*

What have the faults or sins of men to do with your obligations to yourself, to the world, to the church, and to God?

166. *Is it harmful to wear needless adornment, such as jewelry and costly array?*

Christians should so dress as to show that their minds are occupied with nobler objects. Their external appear-ance should evince *gravity, simplicity, decency,* and *mod-*

esty. They should dress neatly, plainly, and suitably to persons professing godliness. Dr. Adam Clarke says: "Were religion out of the question, common sense would say, Be decent, be moderate and modest." We by no means claim that plainness in dress and freedom from needless adornment constitute a Christian.

167. *Is the use of tobacco to be condemned?*

It is. We are divinely commanded to "deny ourselves," to "keep the body under," to "abstain from all appearance of evil," and to "cleanse ourselves from *all filthiness* of the *flesh* and spirit." The Christian's body is a "temple of the Holy Ghost," and he has no right to pollute it with any thing *filthy* or *poisonous.*

168. *Has the world ever regarded the Bible standard of religion as otherwise than fanatical?*

This blind and wicked world has always accounted religion as madness and frenzy. The apostles were called "babblers" and "fools," and said to be "mad," "drunk," and "beside themselves." Christ was accused of being possessed of devils. Luther was styled a heretic. Wesley, Whitefield, and their coadjutors, were called fools, fanatics, and enthusiasts.

The verdict of an English jury was: "We find and present Charles Wesley to be a person of ill fame, a vagabond, and a common disturber of his Majesty's peace, and we pray he may be transported."

169. *What was the fate of those who presented Christianity in its primitive, unsullied purity?*

To pave the way for a work of blood, this ungodly world cruelly murdered God's innocent and lovely Son—drove him out of the world.

1. Matthew is supposed to have suffered martyrdom by the sword at a city in Ethiopia.

2. Mark was dragged through the streets of Alexandria, in Egypt, until he expired.

3. Luke was hanged upon an olive-tree in Greece.

4. John was put into a caldron of boiling oil, at Rome, and escaped death. He afterward died a natural death at Ephesus in Asia.

5. James the Great, after suffering great persecution, was beheaded at Jerusalem.

6. James the Less was thrown from a pinnacle, or wing of the temple, and then beaten to death with a fuller's club.

7. Philip was hanged up against a pillar at Hierapolis, a city of Phrygia.

8. Bartholomew was flayed alive by the command of a barbarous king.

9. Andrew was bound to a cross, where he preached to the people till he expired.

10. Thomas was run through the body by a lance near Malipar, in the East Indies.

11. Jude was shot to death with arrows.

12. Simon Zelotes was crucified in Persia.

13. Matthias was first stoned, and afterward beheaded.

14. Peter was crucified with his head downward.

15. Paul, the last and chief of the apostles, also died by violence. He was beheaded at Rome.

170. *What is real fanaticism?*

It is expecting *results* without the use of *proper means.* God has joined the end and the means together, and it is fatally fanatical to expect *pardon, holiness,* and *heaven,* without *prayer, repentance, faith,* and *obedience.* Fanaticism is being governed by *imagination,* rather than by *judgment.*

171. *Does the Bible countenance shouting and praising the Lord with a loud voice?*

The Bible says: *"For the whole multitude of the disciples began to praise God with a loud voice."* "If these should hold their peace, the *stones* would immediately cry out." "Oh, *clap* your *hands, all* ye people; *shout* unto God with the voice of triumph."

A striking and beautiful variety is seen in the effects of the miracles of Christ and of the apostles. Blind Bartimæus, after he was healed, followed Jesus giving *glory to God.* Simon Peter's wife's mother, after she was healed, went about her *domestic duties.* The man who lived in the tombs, possessed of the devil, after he was healed, *sat down* at Jesus' feet, clothed and in his right mind. At the transfiguration of Christ, Peter and John *fell on their faces,* and declared it was good for them to be there. After the poor cripple, lying at the gate called Beautiful, was healed, he *leaped* and *praised* God. Peter did not reprove him nor stop him, but he let him try his new strength; he had been a poor cripple all his life.

172. *Does the Bible countenance responses in religious worship?*

It does. "And Ezra blessed the Lord, the great God. And ALL the PEOPLE answered, *Amen,* AMEN." "Blessed be the Lord God of Israel from everlasting to everlasting; and *let all the people* say AMEN." "How shall he that occupieth the room of the unlearned say, *Amen,* at thy giving of thanks, seeing he understandeth not what thou sayest?"

173. *Does the Bible countenance physical prostration, and what may appear to carnal men as confusion?*

Paul and Silas were charged with turning the world upside down, and we presume they did not deny the charge. When God met Abraham, and made the great promise to him, *"Abraham fell on his face and laughed."* Although he *"fell* on his *face* and *laughed,"* yet the apostle says, "He staggered not at the promise of God through unbelief, but was strong in faith, giving *glory* to God." The Psalmist says: "When the Lord turned again the captivity of Zion, we were like them that *dream.* Then was our *mouth filled with laughter,* and our *tongue* with *singing.*"

174. *Are bodily prostrations and physical exercises any part of religion?*

They are not; but they often accompany the mighty outpouring of the Spirit and work of God.

President Charles G. Finney says: "It is very plain that bodily prostrations and agitations are no part of religion. But it is just as plain that these may be the *natural effect* of discoveries of religious truth. Several instances of bodily prostration and agitations are recorded in the Bible as the result of such discoveries.

President Jonathan Edwards' ministry was blessed with one of the mightiest outpourings of the Holy Spirit that has ever taken place on this continent.

In speaking of it, he says: "It was a *very frequent* thing to see a house full of *outcries, faintings, convulsions,* and *such like,* both with *distress* and with *admiration* and *joy.* There were some instances of persons *lying in a sort of trance* [what the old Methodists called having the power], remaining for perhaps a whole twenty-four hours motionless, and with their senses locked up, but in the mean time under strong imaginations, as though they went to heaven, and had there a vision of glorious and delightful objects.

He says, in speaking of a revival in Scotland in 1625, that "it was then a frequent thing for many to be so extraordinarily seized with terror in the hearing of the word, by the Spirit of God convincing them of sin, that they fell down, and were carried out of the church, who afterward proved most solid and lively Christians. Many in Ireland, in time of a great outpouring of the Spirit there in 1628, were so *filled with divine comforts,* and a sense of God, that they had but little use of either meat, drink, or sleep, and professed that they did not feel the need thereof."

175. *Is it right to pray for bodily exercise?*

We think it dangerous to either desire, expect, or pray for any physical demonstrations. It is our duty to pray for the mighty cleansing power of the Holy Spirit, and let God work in his own way.

176. *What is our safeguard against delusions and imaginations?*

The *Bible.* This is our only standard of doctrine and experience. We are to be Bible Christians. We should keep close to the word of God, and never suppose that any measure of the Holy Spirit obtainable in this world will supersede the teachings of the blessed Bible. God's revealed word is the voice of the Spirit; and the more completely our hearts are filled, subdued, and kept in the Spirit, the more perfectly we shall understand the Bible, and be able to live according to its letter and spirit.

177. *Should the sanctified soul seek, expect, or desire any thing beyond more holiness—as gifts, new revelations?*

By no means. The heart *full* of *love* has already found "a more excellent way" than these.

Mr. Wesley says: "Another ground of these and a thousand mistakes is, the not considering deeply that *love is the highest gift of God—humble, gentle, patient love;* that all *visions, revelations, manifestations* whatever, are *little things* compared to *love;* and that all the gifts above mentioned are either the same with, or infinitely inferior to it.

SECTION XXI

178. *What advice would you give those professing holiness?*

1. Keep up a daily, or rather a perpetual, devotement of all to God. *"Submit yourselves, therefore, to God."*

2. Remember the life of the Christian is a life of faith. We are *justified* by faith, *sanctified* by faith, and must *stand* by faith. There must be a continuous faith.

3. You must acquire the habit of living by the minute. Take care of the present moment. Trust God *now;* do God's will *now;* do not offend God *now.*

4. Live in the constant use of all the ordinary and instituted means of grace—public and private prayer, meditation, searching the Scriptures, and the sacrament. *"They that wait upon the Lord shall renew their strength; they shall mount up with wings as eagles; they shall run, and not be weary; and they shall walk, and not faint."*

5. Do everything in the name of the Lord Jesus, and to the glory of God.

6. Avoid sinful *lightness* and *levity* on the one hand, or *moroseness* on the other. Be cheerful, but not frivolous and vain; sorrowful, but not sour or gloomy.

7. Cultivate the deepest humility and reverence in your approaches and addresses to God.

8. Study the Bible. Be a Bible Christian in *theory,* in *experience,* and in *practice.* Make your *honesty, justice, veracity,* and *self-denial* harmonize with the teaching of the Bible. Avoid seeking, or encouraging others to seek any mystical experience not explicitly taught in the Bible.

9. Redeem your time. Imitate the example of Christ:

rise early in the morning, and while others are slumbering, pray, "search the Scriptures," and commune *with* God.

10. Acquire the habit of constant watchfulness against sin. *"Therefore let us not sleep, as do others; but let us watch and be sober."*

11. You must absolutely refuse to comply with temptation, under any circumstances, or to any degree. In the strength of God you must say No to the tempter every time.

12. Endeavor to preserve a perfect consistency between your *profession* and *practice*. *"I beseech you that ye walk* WORTHY *of the vocation wherewith ye are called."*

13. Be careful how you consider *impulses* and *impressions* as the teachings of the Spirit. We are to be "led by the Spirit," but it is principally by its illuminations.

14. Read the best writers on Christian holiness. But the Bible should be *first, last,* and *always*. *"Give attendance to reading, to exhortation, to doctrine."*

15. Do not let the adversary lead you to dwell upon some *one subject*, to the exclusion of others, such as *faith, dress, pride, worldliness, masonry*. The Bible has no hobby but *"holiness without which no man shall see the Lord."*

16. Be careful and not *underestimate* or *disparage* justification and regeneration. It is a *great* and *glorious* thing to become a child of God, and an heir of eternal life. *"Walking in all the commandments and ordinances of the Lord blameless."*

17. Avoid an unwarrantable extreme in allowing this *one* subject to become *entirely absorbing*.

18. In the confession of holiness avoid all *ostentation, display,* and *affection*. Let your testimony be artless, simple, easy; let it exalt Christ, and humble you. *"Let your speech be always with grace seasoned with salt,*

that ye may know how ye ought to answer every man."

19. Do not seek to be *conspicuous*. Seek no prominence because of your learning, talents, piety, person, or possessions.

20. On the other hand, do not (through a desire to avoid being conspicuous) neglect to "stand up for Jesus."

21. Avoid all evil speaking. Never talk about the faults of an absent person. Watch over your lips, and *"speak evil of no man."*

Good !

22. Do not allow yourself to talk much about the *opposition* you meet with from ministers and Christians. Never pray for yourself or others as if you or they were persecuted, especially not in public.

23. Avoid a censorious, fault-finding spirit. This will sour and ruin your soul. You may *grieve,* but never *fret.* You may *sorrow* over the condition of things, but do not scold.

Good !

24. Be careful to treat with the utmost kindness those who have not obtained this rich experience. Do not fall out with them on account of their dullness to learn or their slowness to believe, and unwillingness to seek holiness.

SECTION XXII

179. *Where has the doctrine of Christian perfection been in the past history of the church that we seem only to hear of it now?*

It is as old as the Bible, and some parts of the Bible are nearly four thousand years old. It is taught and enforced in the moral law given at Sinai to the Israelites. When Abraham was ninety years old, the Lord appeared unto him, and said, "I am the Almighty God; walk before me, and be thou perfect." This is proof that this doctrine was inculcated four hundred years before the giving of the law.

That the Apostolic Fathers, Martrys, and primitive Christians believed in, and walked in the light of this grace, is very evident. They lived and died abiding in Christ, under the cleansing blood of the atonement. It was this grace that gave them their great success, and afforded them sustaining power in the jaws of death. Ignatius, bishop of Antioch, who was given to the wild beasts at Rome when one hundred and seven years of age, said, "I thank thee, O Lord, that thou hast vouchsafed to honor me with a perfect love towards thee."

When threatenings were sent to Chrysostom from the hand of the Empress, he replied, *"Go tell Eudoxia that I fear nothing but sin."*

Irenæus taught that those were perfect "who present soul, body, and spirit faultless to the Lord. Therefore those are perfect who have the spirit and perseverance of God, and have preserved their souls and bodies without fault."

119

Clement, in his Epistle to the Ephesians, says: "Ye see, then, beloved, how great and wonderful a thing love is, and that no words can declare its perfection. Let us beseech Christ that we may live in love unblamable."

Macarius taught the doctrine more clearly than any of the Fathers. Of our duty and privilege, he says: "It is *perfect purity from sin,* freedom from all shameful lusts and passions, and the assumption of perfect virtue; that is, the purification of the heart by the plenary and experimental communion of the perfect and divine Spirit."

180. *Did not the doctrine of Christian perfection originate with Mr. Wesley and the Methodist Church?*

By no means. The outlines of this doctrine and experience, as we have seen, can be culled from the writings of the best divines from the time of Christ. Mr. Wesley and his coadjutors taught it as they found it in the Bible and experienced it in their own hearts. The essential elements of the Wesleyan doctrine have been developed from the earliest ages of the church in proportion as vital Christianity has prevailed. Every great evangelist since the apostles, who has made his mark on his age, has taught the doctrine with more or less distinctness.

In France, in 1620, it was taught by Molinos, who suffered imprisonment and death for this scriptural truth. It was then called *mysticism,* or *Quietism.* Archbishop Fenelon, a French bishop, taught the experience in all its essential items, though he mixed with it much of error and human merit.

Madam Guyon was clear in the experience, and for her devotion to God and His truth was imprisoned in the French Bastille for four years.

George Fox, the founder of the society called Friends, taught that it was the privilege of Christians to be fully saved from sin, and was imprisoned and greatly persecuted for teaching and professing Christian holiness nearly a hundred years before the Wesleys began to preach it.

Samuel Rutherford, more than two hundred years ago, said: "Christ is more to be loved for giving us sanctification than justification. It is in some respects greater love in him to sanctify than to justify, for he maketh us more like himself in his own essential portraiture and image in sanctification."

In the ritual of the Protestant Episcopal church we have the following: "Cleanse the thoughts of our hearts by the inspiration of the Holy Spirit, that we may *perfectly love thee,* and worthily magnify thy holy name, through Jesus Christ our Lord." . . . "Vouchsafe to *keep us this day without sin,* and grant thy people grace to withstand the temptations of the world, the flesh, and the devil, and *with pure hearts* and minds to follow thee."

No Christian in the world would hesitate to offer these prayers, and yet they are perfectly accordant with the doctrine of Christian perfection, and a perpetual indorsement of this doctrine in the most solemn spiritual services of that church.

Soon after our war with England there was a mighty outpouring of the Spirit, and thousands of believers entered into the rest of perfect love. At that period Bishop Asbury wrote in his journal: "Our pentecost has come for sanctification. I have good reason to believe, that upon the eastern shore of Maryland four thousand have been converted since the first of May, and a thousand sanctified." Rev. Henry Bœhm gives an account of some of the work at this time, in his dairy. (See question 136.)

During this period it was extensively written upon, and special meetings for its promotion were started in several of our chief cities, and many entered into the experience. Mrs. Phœbe Palmer was an honored instrument in the hands of God in promoting this work. During forty years, a special service has been held each week at her residence in New York, and Christians of all lands and all sects have visited this meeting, and been led into the King's highway of perfect love.

She and her devoted husband traveled extensively in Canada, in England, and all through our own country, teaching the doctrine of full redemption through faith in the blood of Christ; and God made her an evangelist of light and love to thousands and tens of thousands on both sides of the Atlantic. She gave constant prominence to this experience, and her spirit was fragrant with its *sweetness* and *power*.

During this period Rev. Charles G. Finney, president of Oberlin College, and Professor Mahan, of the Congregational Church, experienced this grace, taught it to their theological students, and wrote much upon the subject. For years Oberlin College sent out but few young men to the ministry who did not either profess or believe in this doctrine. Although President Finney mixed the doctrine with some new-school Calvinistic sentiments, yet in the great essentials he harmonized with the Wesleyan view.

181. *Do not the formation of associations, and holding special meetings for the promotion of holiness, tend to division in the church?*

No legitimate efforts to promote holiness tend to *division among Christians.* The direct opposite of this is true. Sin *alienates* and *divides;* holiness *unites* and *binds* together, and constitutes the strongest bond of union in the church of God. Any other union in the church is but a rope of sand.

Holding special meetings for the promotion of holiness, and pressing it upon the attention of the church by associations, organized only for mutual co-operation in such work, will create division *only where it ought to*—among *dead, worldly* professors, who attend *theaters, parlor dances, festivals, places of amusement,* and *play euchre,* and yet belong to the church, and desire to run it on the line of their *spirit* and *lives.* Proud, fashionable, and worldly people in the church, annoyed by those deeply devoted to God, have made this cry from the days of Wesley.

SECTION XXIII

182. *Is not the church subject to many and great dangers?*

She is; and in view of it needs holiness as a coat of mail and a strong tower, to secure her safety. She has frightful dangers in her outward prosperity. She has dangers in her accumulation of wealth and numbers, and in her increasing popular and secular power; and unless her purity and moral power are kept *clear* and *strong*, she will inevitably meet with sad and deplorable reverses.

When the Methodist Church, or any other church, relies for her success upon any thing but deep, vital, and practical godliness, she will inevitably fail in accomplishing her great mission. Numbers, wealth, learning, position, or popularity, can never supply the place of *piety*. This is indispensable, and it must be *first, last,* and *always*.

There is a want of men who fearlessly apply the great law of God, and the law of love, to all the vices of the age, and the time-serving, worldly tendencies of the church. These are not the dreams of a morbid fancy, or the suggestions of an uncharitable judgment; would they were either, rather than the painful truth. We are aware there are many precious exceptions—many thousands who are true to God, and are ready to meet and bear a baptism of blood, if need be, for the cause of Christ; but still facts enough are before our eyes to prompt, press, and push the questions: How many professed Christians participate with the ungodly in vain amusements? How

124

many follow, and how many even lead in extravagant
equipage and worldly follies? How many do business on
principles which will not bear the light of Bible morality?
"LOVE THY NEIGHBOR AS THYSELF." It must be seen the
world is yet far from being in sympathy with Christ, or
in allegiance to His scepter. Truly, *"in the last days per-
ilous times shall come."*

183. *Is it wrong to seek the good opinion of our fellow-
men?*

A modified desire for the good opinions of our fellow-
men, within given bounds, is constitutional, and may not
be wrong, nor displeasing to God: but to *seek* and *receive* the honor and favor of men, rather than that of
God, indicates spiritual blindness and contempt for God.

The great evil of this state of mind is seen in the declaration of Christ: "How can ye believe, which receive
honor one of another, and seek not the honor which
cometh from God only?" This question of Christ implies
the strongest form of negation. Worldly attachments,
seeking honors, pride, and ambition exclude faith. They
render it impossible. Faith commits the will and whole
soul to God, and implies a supreme regard for God's
views, authority, and pleasure. Self-love, ambition, and
seeking earthly honors exclude this.

"The fear of man bringeth a snare"; and the desire
to please man and escape public odium for godliness has
overthrown many a professed Christian. Holy men can
no more escape public odium than Christ could. Is the
servant above his Lord? Has the carnality of wicked
men changed? Can we be more wise and prudent than
our Lord? He said: "Woe unto you when all men shall
speak well of you." There should be carefulness, and
wisdom, and we should not recklessly or needlessly excite
opposition or odium; do the best we can, and there will

be plenty of it, without careless provocation on our part. Let us seek the approbation of God first, last, and always, and leave all results with Him.

184. *How is a worldly, compromising spirit manifested?*

In many ways, some of which are the following:

1. In efforts to popularize Christianity with the world, and seeking to increase her influence in that way.

2. In efforts to lower the Bible standard of piety, in order to make it less repulsive to the minds of carnal men.

3. In efforts to *regulate* sin, instead of *opposing* and *prohibiting it.*

4. In acts which *pander* to the vices of wicked men, or which *countenance,* directly or indirectly, the commission of sin.

5. In the abandonment of Bible terms, in the relation of religious experience, in order to please men.

6. In the *polishing* and *softening* of those truths which God has left *rough* and *hard.*

7. In depending for the prosperity of the church upon her wealth and popularity, or upon the learning, talents, and eloquence of her ministers, rather than upon the baptism of the Holy Ghost, and a solid, high tone of piety in her ministry and membership.

The Spirit of God and the spirit of the world can never harmonize. Sin is an offensive, abominable thing, which God hates, and "the carnal mind is enmity against God." There is no sympathy between sin and holiness, and no medium ground for any one to occupy. Jesus said: "No man can serve two masters." "He that is not with me is against me, and he that gathereth not with me scattereth abroad."

Martin Luther said: "I find it impossible to avoid offending guilty men; for there is no way of avoiding it but by our silence, or their patience: and silent we cannot be, because of God's commands; and patient they cannot be, because of their guilt."

185. *Is the baptism with the Holy Ghost, or being filled with the Spirit, the blessing of holiness?*

It includes it. To be *"full* of the Holy Ghost," *full* of faith and the Holy Ghost," *"full* of faith and power," and to be *"filled* with all the *fullness* of God," is to possess full salvation, or perfect love. To be "filled with all the fullness of God," is, however, much more than merely to be sanctified; it involves enlargement and growth in love, power, and holiness.

The one hundred and twenty gathered in the upper room "were all *filled* with the Holy Ghost." That baptism, doubtless, sanctified every one of them. It took all the unbelief out of Thomas. It prepared Stephen for martyrdom. It completely cured Peter, so that he never cowed before the enemies of the Lord, or cursed, or swore, or denied his Lord again. He lived a hero, and died a martyr. He was crucified with his head downward, because he chose not to die like his Lord.

186. *Can those entirely sanctified lose that grace, and still retain a justified relation to God?*

Bishop Foster says: "Not every thing that would mar a perfectly holy character would destroy the filial relation of the believer; as that relation subsisted prior to entire sanctification, so it may remain when that state is marred —ceases. Or the loss of entire sanctification may be attended, or immediately followed, by acts which also utterly destroy the earlier and inferior blessing of justification."—*Christian Purity*, p. 171.

187. *Why need we seek holiness if we can die safe in a justified state?*

"All who are justified," says Rev. J. S. Inskip, "and retain their justification, will undoubtedly be saved. It should, however, be remembered, that justification can be maintained only by going on to entire sanctification." —*Methods of Promoting Perfect Love*, p. 10.

188. *Is not the fact that many persons lose perfect love several times before they become established therein, against the seeking of it?*

It is at least no more so than the same fact in regard to justification is against the seeking of that blessing. Doubtless, if the light of justification were more *general*, and more *clear* in the church, converts would be less likely to lose their justification during their early experience; and if the blessing of perfect love were more generally sought and obtained by the ministry and membership, and more clearly and faithfully preached and exemplified in the pulpit, those who seek and obtain it, would be less likely to lose it during their early experience.

Let sympathy in the church become as general in its favor as it is for justification, and let clear witnesses for entire sanctification become as numerous in the ministry and membership as they should be, and you will hear of but few losing the blessing.

189. *What relation does saving faith sustain to truth?*

It is inseparably connected with it. Saving faith is a practical reception of saving truth, by *submission* to its claims.

190. *Is it vitally important that men have correct views of truth?*

It is; as saving truth is inseparable from salvation. Religious truth sustains the same relation to the soul that food does to the body. Truth received becomes "the power of God unto salvation"; rejected, it becomes "a savor of death unto death." The doctrines of revelation are the life of the soul; the foundation of all experimental and practical religion. "As a man thinketh so is he." Opinions influence conduct, they are the seeds of actions. In the nature of things, religious doctrine must be the base of religion, and a correct Christian creed the foundation of a vigorous and intelligent piety.

191. *What class of people most commonly believe in, and seek full salvation?*

The great mass of Christian people have always been more from the humble walks of life, than from the higher classes, the elevated ranks of life. This is true regarding those who seek and possess full salvation. Divine grace has been most displayed in reforming and purifying the lives of the *common people*. True virtue or excellence, sincerity and amiability, honesty and purity, are usually found most in humble life. God is no respecter of persons, and there is no royal way to his favor, or to heaven. Human distinctions are mainly confined to man and to this world, and human depravity has much to do with them.

No Christian truth or experience depends for its success on human wisdom or greatness, and the work and influence of Christian sanctification is not dependent on any class of men, high or low, great or small, rich or poor. Any religious system built upon human power, wisdom, or wealth, will be confounded and brought to naught. It is only safe to trust in God.

192. *Are worldly amusements sinful?*

All those amusements that cannot be sought or used in the name of the Lord, or to the glory of God, are sinful, and are *insipid* and *corrupting* to devout minds. No Christian needs them, or desires them; he has more important things to engage his time and attention. No

reasonable man sacrifices the more important thing for
the less; and amusements are the least important, and
are generally injurious to morals and spirituality. They
bring religion into unworthy and debasing alliances, and
cripple the aggressive power of the Church. The late
Archbishop Spaulding, of the Roman Catholic Church,
told Dr. J. M. King, of New York, that "the confessional
revealed the fact that nineteen women out of twenty who
had fallen from virtue, dated the first step in the downward career to dancing parties."

The Lord has made ample provision for the healthful
happiness of His children, in the gift of the Holy Ghost,
the *Comforter,* and therefore they do not need amusements, such as *dancing,* games, theaters, and the like,
which worldly people seek.

193. *Are Fairs, Festivals, or Theatricals proper means
of raising money for church purposes?*

No. They are decidedly wrong, and a disgrace to
Christianity. Modern religious theaters, fairs, and festivals, with their whole program of grab-bags, postoffices,
fish-ponds, lotteries, games, and dancing, under church
sanction, are a shame and a curse, and should be abandoned by the whole Church as belonging to the world,
the flesh, and the devil. It may be said of many churches,
in this regard, *"Ye are cursed with a curse."* God wants
no money raised by such means to carry on His work.
The finances of the Christian Church should be conduct-
ed on Christian principles, with common sense, purity,
and honor. A careful observation during a ministry of
thirty years, has convinced us that these modes of raising
money are fruitful of evil, and should be abandoned.

194. *How are entirely sanctified souls to be distin-
guished from those not entirely sanctified?*

In the outward life there is no marked difference, as the distinction is not so much in the outer life as in the inner life and experience. The distinction being one of *moral condition* and not so much in outward life and acts, we are not to look for too much in that respect. The justified and regenerate should live just as correctly in outward conduct as those entirely sanctified. Purity of heart is manifested by being more deeply humble; by greater simplicity and sweetness of spirit; by greater strength of faith, and by living more "soberly, righteous-ly, and godly in this present world"; in short, by being more like Christ.

Good!

195. *What has become of indwelling sin, in those entirely sanctified?*

It has not only been conquered, as is the case with all regenerate souls, but has been exterminated. In the entirely sanctified soul inbred sin is not merely suppressed, or conquered, but is cast out. The soul is cleansed, and when the devil comes he finds nothing in it but what is in harmony with God—the *"evil treasure"* having been expelled. The Saviour said, "Satan cometh and hath nothing in me"; and, "As he is, so are we in this world."

196. *Should the regeneration of sinners and the sanctification of believers go on together?*

Such we believe to be the true order of God. Salvation must come out of Zion. The church is to obtain and impart life. The sanctification of believers in the church, and the conversion of sinners out of it, should go on simultaneously. Mr. Wesley said, for each believer sanctified ten sinners would be converted. Nothing adds such power to a revival as to have believers sanctified while sinners are being converted.

The best, easiest, and the most extensive and lasting revivals are those which commence with the "perfecting of the saints." Such reformations move easily and powerfully, and go deep and thorough in saving souls. This was true of the powerful and extensive revivals under the labors of Wesley, Bramwell, Hunter, Carvosso, Stoner, Abbott, Hibbard, Garrettson, Caughey, Finney, and Mrs. Phœbe Palmer.

The sanctification of believers constitutes the best possible preparation the church can possess for the reception of converts to her bosom. It is to be feared many, very many, genuine converts have been ruined by uniting with *cold, worldly,* and *unsanctified churches.* The church of God carries a fearful responsibility in this matter.

197. *How much ought I to fast?*

Your body is the "temple of the Holy Ghost," and you are to *govern* it, but not to *injure* it. You should *fast* enough to make it a means of grace, but not so much as to make it an instrument of temptation. The state of your health will help you to decide this question.

198. *Does the Lord ever heal the body supernaturally in answer to prayer?*

He does. While "the age of miracles is past," in so far as attesting the divinity of the gospel, it is not past as it respects *Divine interposition* and *supernatural* power in answer to prayer. The rationalist and skeptic may doubt and cavil, while the devoted Christian believes and knows that God answers prayer. We believe in special interpositions of providence and prayer cures.

The Scripture warrant for prayer is as boundless as *human necessity,* and the limits of prayer are only the Divine wisdom and will. (See Exod. 15:26; Exod. 23:25; Matt. 21:22; John 15:7; Psalm 103:3; James 5:15; I John 5:14; Matt. 7:11; Luke 11:9.)

199. *What evidences indicate the guidance of the Holy Spirit?*

1. A clearer view of the truth. The Holy Spirit is to teach men, and lead them into the truth.

2. An increased quickness and power of conscience, and an increasing activity of the moral sense.

3. An increasing calmness and peace in all the natural sensibilities, producing quietness of mind.

4. An increasing light in the providential dealings of God.

5. An increasing sentiment of propriety, decency, and good sense, such as modesty, courteousness, and gentleness of manner.

6. An increasing tendency to glorify God.

200. *What evidences indicate advancement in holiness?*

1. An increasing comfort and delight in the holy Scriptures.

2. An increasing interest in prayer, and an increasing spirit of prayer.

3. An increasing desire for the holiness of others.

4. A more heart-searching sense of the value of time.

5. Less desire to hear, see, and know for mere curiosity.

6. A growing inclination against magnifying the faults and weaknesses of others, when obliged to speak of their characters.

7. A greater readiness to speak freely to those who do not enjoy religion, and to backward professors of religion.

8. More disposition to glory in reproach for Christ's sake, and suffer, if need be, for him.

9. An increasing tenderness of conscience, and being more scrupulously conscientious.

10. Less affected by changes of place and circumstances.

11. A sweeter enjoyment of the holy Sabbath, and the services of the sanctuary.

12. An increasing love for the searching means of grace.

201. *What is the grand secret of holy living?*

It is to *obtain* and *retain* the *perpetual presence, fullness,* and *illumination* of the Holy Ghost. "*He shall abide with you for ever.*"

THE AUTHOR'S EXPERIENCE

202. *Will you relate your experience of regeneration, and of entire sanctification?*

I will. The Saviour's precious love constrains me to testify to His gracious dealings with my soul at every suitable opportunity.

In May, 1858, I was appointed to Court Street Church, Binghamton, and went there much prejudiced against the professors of holiness in that church; and they were, doubtless, prejudiced against me, as they had cause to believe I would oppose them. I soon found in my pastoral visitations, that where those persons lived who professed the blessing of holiness, there I felt the most of divine influence and power, and realized a liberty in prayer, and an access to God in those families, which I did not elsewhere.

Let me remark, while I was prejudiced against holiness as a *distinct* blessing, and against its *special* advocates, I did desire and believe in a deep, thorough, vital piety, and was ready to sympathize with it wherever I found it. I had attended prayer and class meetings but few times before I saw clearly that there were those in that society whose experience and piety possessed a *richness, depth,* and *power* which I had not; and that I was preaching to some who enjoyed more religion than their pastor.

The better I became acquainted with them, the more I was convinced of this, and the more deeply I became convicted of my remaining depravity and need of being cleansed in the blood of Christ. I also became convinced that those professors of holiness were Wesleyan in their faith, experience, and practice, while I had drifted away somewhat from the Bible and Wesleyan theory of Christian perfection.

Through the entire summer of 1858 I was seeking holiness, but kept the matter to myself. During this time none of the professors of holiness said any thing to me on the subject, but, as I have learned since, were praying for me night and day. God only knew the severe struggles I had that long summer, during many hours of which I lay on my face in my study, begging Jesus to cleanse my poor, unsanctified heart; and yet was unwilling to make a public avowal of my feelings, or to ask the prayers of God's people for my sanctification.

The Binghamton district campmeeting commenced that year the first day of September, and about eighty of the members of my charge attended it with me. During six days of the meeting, the sanctification of my soul was before my mind constantly, and yet I neither urged others to seek it, nor intimated to any one my convictions and struggles on the subject. Six days of such deep humiliation, severe distress, and hard struggles I never endured before.

A number of the members present from my charge had once enjoyed this grace, and had lost it. Some who professed to enjoy it were becoming silent upon the subject. With but very few exceptions, we, as a church, were practically staving off and ignoring the doctrine and duty of entire sanctification. The Lord was evidently displeased with us, and so shut us up that our prayer meetings, in our large society tent, literally ran out. The brethren and sisters became afflicted with themselves, and afflicted with each other. Some of them were even tempted to strike their tents and go home.

On the last day of the meeting, a few minutes before preaching, a faithful member of the church came to me weeping, and said, "Brother Wood, there is no use in trying to dodge this question. You know your duty. If you will lead the way, and define your position as a seeker of entire sanctification, you will find that many of the members of your charge have a mind to do the same." The Lord had so humbled my heart that I was willing to do any thing to obtain relief. After a few moments' reflection I replied, "Immediately after preaching I will appoint a meeting in our tent on the subject of holiness, and will ask the prayers of the church for my own soul."

Glory be to God! the Rubicon was passed. The moment of decision was the moment of triumph. In an instant I felt a giving away in my heart, so sensible and powerful, that it appeared physical rather than spiritual; a moment after I felt an indescribable sweetness permeating my entire being. It was a sweetness as real and as sensible to my soul as ever the sweetest honey to my taste. I immediately walked up into the stand. Just as the preacher gave out his text, Ecclesiastes 12:13, "Let us hear the conclusion of the whole matter," the baptism of fire and power came upon me.

For me to describe what I then realized is utterly impossible. It was such as I need not attempt to describe to those who have felt and tasted it, and such as I can not describe to the comprehension of those whose hearts have never realized it. I was conscious that Jesus had me in His arms, and that the Heaven of heavens was streaming through and through my soul in such beams of light and overwhelming love and glory, as can never be uttered. *The half can never be told!*

It was like marching through the gates of the city to the bosom of Jesus, and taking a full draught from the river of life.

Hallelujah! Glory! glory! I have cause to shout over the work of that precious hour.

It was a memorable era in the history of my probation, a glorious epoch in my religious experience—*never,* NEVER to be forgotten. Jesus there and then—all glory to His blessed name!—sweetly, completely, and most powerfully sanctified my soul and body to Himself. He *melted, cleansed, filled,* and *thrilled* my feeble, unworthy soul with holy, sin-consuming power.

Glory be to God! Perfect love is the *richest,* the *sweetest,* and the *purest* love this side of Paradise. Angels have nothing better. Well may the poet sing:

> "Oh, for this love let rocks and hills
> Their lasting silence break,
> And all harmonious human tongues
> The Saviour's praises speak!"

I had always been much prejudiced against persons losing their strength; consequently, as might be expected, when the Holy Ghost came upon me in the stand, surrounded by some thirty preachers and three thousand people, it was God's order to take control of both body and soul, and swallow me up in the great deep of his presence and power.

After about three hours I regained sufficient strength to walk to the tent, and we commenced a meeting for the promotion of holiness. I told my church my purpose to ask their prayers as a seeker of holiness, but that Jesus had forestalled my design by accepting my soul the moment I consented to stand up for holiness, and was willing to be anything or do anything to obtain it.

A willingness to humble myself, and take a decided stand for holiness, and face opposition to it in the church,

and take the odium of being an advocate of holiness in Binghamton, where that doctrine had been trailing in the dust for years, constituted the turning-point with me. After I reached that point of complete submission, I had no consciousness of making any special effort in believing; my whole being seemed simply, and without effort, to be borne away to Jesus.

Our meeting continued all night; and such a night I never experienced. A large number of my leading members commenced seeking holiness; and about every half hour during that whole night the glorious power of God came down from the upper ocean in streams as sweet as heaven. At times it was unspeakable and almost unendurable. It was *oppressively* sweet—a *weight of glory*.

Every time the power of God came, one or more souls entered the land of Beulah, the Canaan of perfect love. Some shouted, some laughed, some wept, and a large number lay prostrate from three to five hours, beyond the power of shouting or weeping. Hallelujah to the great God! those present will never forget that night of refining and sanctifying power.

What I received at the time Jesus sanctified my soul was only a drop in the bucket compared to what it has since pleased Him to impart. From that hour the deep and solid communion of my soul with God, and the rich baptisms of love and power, have been "unspeakable, and full of glory."

> "Oh, matchless bliss of perfect love!
> It lifts me up to things above;
>   It bears on eagles' wings;
> It gives my ravished soul a feast,
> And makes me here a constant guest,
>   With Jesus, priests, and kings."

With the blessed *doctrine* and *experience* of *purity*, I am more and more impressed, charmed, and satisfied.

Under its quickening power and light, I am amazed, humbled, and delighted. Oh, that I may enjoy it more fully, live it more perfectly, and preach and teach it more clearly, and in every way, by *tongue,* and *pen,* and *life,* do more for its promotion! I expect to preach it as long as I preach any thing, and when I cease preaching it, expect to be in heaven. In looking over these twenty-one years, I see much to humble me in the dust.

I might have written much more in regard to my weakness, unworthiness, and imperfections, and would have done so, had I supposed it would honor Christ more than to write about the fullness of His grace, and the riches of His love. I have tried with all humility to look to God for guidance, and have felt His blessing resting upon me while writing.